STRESS FRACTURES

Charles R. Swindoll

Stress Fractures

ZondervanPublishingHouse

Grand Rapids, Michigan

A Division of HarperCollinsPublishers

Stress Fractures © *1990 by Charles R. Swindoll, Inc. All rights reserved*

All requests for information should be addressed to: Zondervan Publishing House
Grand Rapids, Michigan 49530

Library of Congress Cataloging-in-Publication Data

Swindoll, Charles R.
    Stress fractures: advice and encouragement for handling your fast-paced life/
Charles R. Swindoll. p. cm. Originally published: Portland, Or. : Multnomah,
c1990. Includes bibliographical references.
    ISBN 0-310-49741-8 (pbk.)
      1. Christian life—1960- 2. Stress (Psychology)—Religious aspects—
Christianity. I. Title.
    BV4501.2.S8965   1994
    248.8'6—dc20   94-2776
                                                          CIP

Unless otherwise indicated, all Scripture references are from the New American
Standard Bible, copyright The Lockman Foundation 1960, 1962, 1963, 1968, 1971,
1972, 1973, 1975, 1977. Used by permission.

Scripture references marked TLB are from The Living Bible, copyright 1971 by
Tyndale House Publishers, Wheaton, Ill. Used by permission.

Scripture references marked Amplified are from The Amplified New Testament,
copyright 1954, 1958 by The Lockman Foundation. Used by permission.

Scripture references marked NIV are from the Holy Bible, New International Version,
copyright 1973, 1978, 1984 by the International Bible Society. Used by permission of
Zondervan Publishing House. All rights reserved.

Scripture references marked KJV are from the Holy Bible: Authorized King James
Version.

Printed in the United States of America.

      98 99 / ❖ DH / 10 9 8 7 6 5

I dedicate this book to the men and women
who serve as our Board of Directors at Insight for Living.
Each one is a splendid model of the qualities
our ministry upholds: faithfulness, integrity, commitment,
and excellence. Their fierce loyalty to Cynthia
and me personally, mixed with their unswerving love
for God and His world, have bonded our hearts together,
creating a stress-free environment that has made these
years we have worked together an ongoing delight.

Intensive Care

Spiritual Therapy

INTRODUCTION

My editor, Larry Libby, had just finished two weeks of intensive computer work on the book you now hold in your hands. Secreted away in a tiny office off his garage, he leaned back in his chair as the orange of an Oregon sunset splashed through a narrow, cobwebbed window. He was pleased with his labors—compiling, sorting, checking, and double-checking. The manuscript was completed, and on deadline. All that was left now was to make a backup copy and take it to the office.

What he had intended to do was erase some old files on the disks and make room for the new files he had labeled "STRESS." That's what he intended. But that's not what he did.

Instead, he typed in a command that erased the whole book. *Are you sure?* the computer asked him. Yes, he was sure.

As quick as a click, it was gone. All of it. Two weeks of work, including a Saturday when he could have flown a kite with his kids. Two weeks of peering into the amber glow of a computer screen. Two weeks of honing, finetuning, and formatting. Gone with the wind. Gone to that twilight zone where all erased computer messages exist in perpetual limbo.

He stared dumbly at the screen, like a calf staring at a new gate.

And then Larry got sick.

Desperately, he lunged at the keyboard and hammered in a directory command, to see what remained on the disk. Other than one single, mocking message, the screen was as clean as an early morning snowy field. The message on his screen simply said, STRESS: NO FILE FOUND.

My friend was experiencing a stress fracture.

Consult a medical book, and it will tell you that stress fractures have to do with microscopic cracks in bones. Consult an engi-

9

neering manual, and it will tell you that stress fractures have to do
with hidden, hairline fissures in bridges and pillars and foundations. Consult your daily life, however, and you'll acknowledge that
the constant stress and pressure you've been enduring has pro-
duced fractures of an entirely different sort.

You're hurting, and you can't explain why.

You have wounds, but you couldn't say where.

You're desperate for help and healing, but you have no idea
where to find it.

You feel so pressed and pulled, you begin to wonder if you'll
break in two and drop like one of those engines on a DC-10.

Stress fractures.

The medical definition offers some insight. Stress fractures
occur, says *Black's Medical Dictionary*, after an undue amount of
exercise . . . "an amount of exercise which an individual is not capable of coping with in his or her state of training. The main feature
is pain over the affected bone. This is usually insidious in onset,
and worse at night. . . ."[1]

A *Sports Illustrated* article painted the picture this way: "A
stress fracture begins when the shocks and strains of playing game
after game create microscopic cracks in the outer layers of bone—
usually in the legs and feet. If the pounding continues and those
tiny crevices, which often go undetected, aren't allowed to heal,
they can enlarge. When the cracks become large enough to cause
pain, they are stress fractures."[2]

Breaks in bones are painful, but can they match the ache of
a fractured spirit . . . or a broken heart? Perhaps you've felt that
kind of pain recently. A pain that lies deep. A pain that haunts you
through the day and throbs into the night.

Some people try to deaden the pang with chemicals or
booze . . . or try to silence its insistent voice with loud music or
constant noise and activity. Ah, but in those rare moments of
silence, when the music is gone and the crowd is quiet, it comes
right back, doesn't it?

Did you ever think of that pain as a friend? As a warning?

"On November 7, 1986, 12,666 people in Portland's
Memorial Coliseum saw Sam Bowie catch the ball at the low post

on the right side of the key, pivot and go up for a jump shot. As Bowie left the floor, those sitting near the court heard a sickening crack. By the time he landed, his right shinbone was all but sticking through his skin."[3]

Bowie had a stress fracture that suddenly became a compound fracture. He'd ignored the dull pain in his right leg for weeks, knowing how NBA coaches and owners tend to look unsympathetically at high-paid athletes who complain of injuries that don't show up on an X-ray. Big Sam's neglect, however, ended his season . . . and might have ended his career.

Let me pass along some good news. Your stress fractures don't have to go on hurting. You don't have to turn to noise, drugs, alcohol, or an extra-marital affair to cope with the pressure you've been enduring. You don't have to push yourself until something snaps with a sickening crack.

This book has some answers that *cannot fail* to bring you relief. I make that statement with confidence, not because of this author's ability, but because of the unfailing, infallible source from which I draw. I speak of our great and gracious God and His eternal Word, the Bible.

Just as there is purpose in your fractures, there is also peace in your future, my friend. Peace and encouragement and perspective and a hope big enough to carry you along from this very day through the rest of your life. It's all in His Word, and it's there for you.

No fracture is too deep for Him to detect or too hidden for Him to heal.

Chuck Swindoll

PART ONE

INTENSIVE CARE

CHAPTER ONE

STRESS

Whoever dubbed our times "The Aspirin Age" didn't miss it very far. It is correct to assume there has never been a more stress-ridden society than ours. For many, gone are the days of enjoying bubbling brooks along winding pathways or taking long strolls near the beach. The relaxed bike ride through the local park has been replaced with the roar of a motorcycle whipping through busy traffic. The easy-come, easy-go lifestyle of the farm has been preempted by a hectic urban family going in six different directions . . . existing on instant dinners, shouting matches, strained relationships, too little sleep, and too much television.

Add financial setbacks, failure at school, unanswered letters, obesity, loneliness, a ringing telephone, unplanned pregnancies, fear of cancer, misunderstanding, materialism, alcoholism, drugs, and an occasional death; then subtract the support of the family unit, divide by dozens of opinions, multiply by 365 days a year, and you have the makings of madness! Stress has become a way of life; it is the rule rather than the exception.

This chapter is designed to help you put a stop to the hurry-worry sindrome. If you will apply its message, you will be well on your way to relief and full recovery.

There is an old Greek motto that says:
> YOU WILL BREAK THE BOW
> IF YOU KEEP IT ALWAYS BENT.

Wise words, but how do we loosen the strings? Even when we make every effort to slow down and relax, others place high demands on us. Their "shoulds" and "oughts" and "musts" hit us like strong gusts of wind, driving our lives onto shallow reefs of frustration—and even despair.

Suicide is now a viable option to many who once would have never tolerated the thought. Every day in the United States, over eighty people take their lives—that's more than three each hour, twenty-four hours every day. The suicide rate for Americans under thirty years of age has increased dramatically in the past decade. For many, the bow has already broken.

A BIBLICAL STRESS CASE

To the surprise of some, the Bible often speaks directly to key issues. Let's step into the time tunnel to find a perfect example of stress. It is the classic story of Mary and Martha, two unmarried sisters whom Jesus visited in their home at Bethany. The account is recorded in the last several verses in Luke 10:

> *Now as they were traveling along, He entered a certain village; and a woman named Martha welcomed Him into her home. And she had a sister called Mary, who moreover was listening to the Lord's word, seated at His feet (vv. 38–39).*

A lovely scene. Jesus dropped by, probably unexpectedly, for a brief visit. Mary, the younger, realized how privileged they were, so she decided to sit down and really make the most of it. She sat at His feet, drinking in His every word.

But Martha? Well, she was neither sitting down nor drinking in. She was under a great deal of stress.

> *But Martha was distracted with all her preparations; and she came up to Him and said, "Lord, do You not care that my sister has left me to do all the serving alone? Then tell her to help me" (v. 40).*

We read that Martha was "distracted." Instead of relaxing and enjoying the Lord's presence, Martha was in a mild frenzy over all her preparations. The lady was trying to fix a nice meal, get everything done on time, arrange the table, and be a good hostess . . . while her sister sat in the room and never offered to help. As her stress reached the point of fracture, Martha reacted strongly.

- She assumed the Lord Jesus didn't care—*"Lord, do You not care . . . ?"*
- She blamed Mary for being irresponsible—*". . . my sister has left me to do all the serving alone . . ."*
- She tried to work things out her way—*". . . tell her to help me."*

It was okay for Martha to want to serve Jesus something to eat. Commendable, in fact. She was like that: active, energetic, diligent, thoughtful, and determined. All fine qualities. But her problem grew out of hand when she attempted to do more than was necessary. She shot a critical glance at her sister because Mary chose not to spend her time in the same way, hustling, bustling, and fussing.

It's interesting that anxiety-prone people frequently blame others for their plight. Rather than realizing their stress is self-appointed, they often criticize others for causing it.

Does that sound unfair? Read on:

> But the Lord answered and said to her, "Martha, Martha, you are worried and bothered about so many things; but only a few things are necessary, really only one, for Mary has chosen the good part, which shall not be taken away from her" (vv. 41–42).

Can't you just hear Jesus? "Marthaaaa . . . Martha!" Then He quickly analyzed her stress in two words—"worried" and "bothered." The term Dr. Luke uses for "worried" is one that means "to be pulled in different directions." The root verb in Greek means "to divide into parts." Martha was being pulled apart from within. Her stress was caused by this internal tearing. A classic case study of a stress fracture! The word *bothered* suggests originally the idea of "noise, tumult, trouble." She was agitated, ripped apart in turmoil.

Unfortunately, it's a familiar sight.

Jesus noticed she was worried and disturbed about "so many things" . . . the meat, the napkins, the timing, the rolls, the setting of the table, the way things looked, the numerous other picky details. She was no longer able to focus on the big picture. The single most important thing she should have chosen got lost in the shuffle. No, there was nothing wrong with her desire to serve Him. Before long, however, worry stole away her perspective. She lost sight of the important.

Charles Hummel calls this "the tyranny of the urgent,"[1] a fitting description. For Martha, who allowed herself to get caught in the sticky web of stress, the important got replaced by the urgent.

THE PERSPECTIVE OF JESUS

The night Jesus was placed under arrest and later subjected to a series of mock trials which ultimately led to His crucifixion, He had been praying to the Father. In that prayer He said: "I glorified Thee on the earth, having accomplished the work which Thou hast given Me to do" (John 17:4).

When you think that through, you will be surprised. He said that He had *completed* the job. Mission accomplished. Yet there were still regions which had not heard. There were still hundreds of blind and sick and lame people as yet untouched and unchanged. There were still millions of slaves in the Roman Empire being mistreated. Yet He said He had accomplished what the Father had for Him to do. Even though there were still numerous needs, our Savior was free of stress. Unlike His nervous friend Martha, Jesus maintained the right perspective.

OVERCOMING WORRY

We have seen a couple of New Testament examples (one negative, the other positive) of people under stress. Let's now go back to the Old Testament and lift out some familiar words of hope to those clenched in the vise-grip of worry.

The following passage is so well known to most Christians

that we have perhaps missed its significant message. Read slowly the words of Solomon:

> *Trust in the* LORD *with all your heart, and do not lean on your own understanding. In all your ways acknowledge Him, and He will make your paths straight (Proverbs 3:5–6).*

Go back and read these words again, please; this time *aloud.*

My Part, God's Part

Let's do a little digging. I'd like to suggest three important observations in what we just read.

First, there are four verbs—words of action—in these two verses:

- trust
- do not lean
- acknowledge
- make straight

A closer look will reveal the first three verbs are commands. They are directed to the child of God, the Christian. They represent our responsibility.

> *Trust . . . do not lean . . . acknowledge. . . .*

The fourth verb is a promise. It declares God's part in the transaction, His responsibility.

> *. . . He will make your paths straight.*

Putting this observation in the form of a simple diagram looks like this:

My Responsibility	*God's Promise*
Trust!	He will make straight . . .
Do not lean!	
Acknowledge!	

A second observation: The same term is used no less than four times. Can you find it? Look again at the verses. Circle the word *your.* God is really emphasizing the personal nature of this truth. He is also telling us we must enter into it individually—no one else can apply it for us.

Your responsibility in your circumstances is to trust with all *your* heart . . . and to refuse to lean on *your* own understanding . . . acknowledging Him in all *your* ways . . . so that He might make straight *your* paths.

Get the picture? Responding to life's situations is *your* choice. No one else can do it for you.

One final observation: The first phrase is linked to the last phrase, giving us the main idea. (Trust . . . He will make straight.) The two middle phrases merely amplify the main idea. (Do not lean . . . acknowledge.) Let me explain.

I am to trust in my Lord without hesitation and without reservation—with all my heart—so that He might step in and take control, making my way meaningful and straight. And what is involved in trusting with all my heart? Two particular decisions: one negative, the other positive.

- Negatively, I am not to lean on my own understanding.
- Positively, I am to acknowledge Him in the whole battleground.

Defining Solomon's Words about Worry

So much for the observations. To make them even more meaningful, let's uncover several of the significant terms.

Trust. At the root of this original Hebrew term is the idea of throwing oneself down and lying extended on the ground, casting all hopes for the present and the future upon another, finding shelter and security there. We are *commanded* by our Lord to cast ourselves fully and absolutely at His feet. Remember: It is with *all* our hearts that we do this.

Heart. Obviously, Solomon is not referring to the organ in the chest that pumps blood. He's using the Hebrew term that appears throughout the Old Testament in reference to one's "inner person" . . . that part of us which is the very center of our intellect, emotion, and will. In other words, we are commanded to cast upon

God our total trust, not holding back in any area of our mind or feeling or volition. No reservations whatsoever.

Understanding. The term appears first in the Hebrew text for the purpose of emphasis: ". . . and upon your understanding do not lean." It is referring to human understanding. The thought is this: "Don't turn first to your own limited viewpoint; don't try to work things out on your own."

Lean. The Hebrew term means "to support oneself, as though leaning for assistance." It's used in Judges 16 where blind Samson leaned on the huge pillars supporting the Philistine temple. Think of resting your weight on a crutch. It's that idea, except it is a *negative* command. "Do not" rest on your own ingenuity. Quit chasing down all the possibilities you can think of. Stay out of the way, guard against fear and panic, scheming and manipulating, worrying and hurrying.

Acknowledge. Here's the positive part. Literally, it means "recognize." In the midst of the whole scene, recognize, mentally call to mind, God's presence and control.

Make straight. It's the thought of making something smooth, straight, right. It includes the idea of removing obstacles that are in the way, as when a road is being built through a mountain pass. The Hebrew verb appears in this verse in a particular stem that denotes intensity. In other words, when the Lord is fully relied upon to handle a given situation, He will do a thorough, complete job of smoothing out our part.

The Swindoll Amplified Version

We've taken a deep look into these verses and examined the vital parts. Now we need to put the thought back together and see the whole picture in a new light.

Throw yourself completely upon the Lord—that is, cast all your present and future needs on Him who is your intimate Savior-God—finding in Him your security and safety. Do this with all your mind and feeling and will. In order to make this possible, you must refuse to support yourself upon the crutch of human ingenuity. Instead, recognize His presence and concern in each one of your circumstances. Then He (having taken full control of the situation) will thoroughly smooth out and straighten your paths, removing each obstacle along the way.

What a magnificent promise to all the "Marthas"—of both sexes—reading this book!

Applying Your Personalized Version

As I think all this through, several specific truths seem to bounce off the pages of Scripture:

- This is a personal promise for anxiety-prone people to claim right now. God has preserved this statement just for you. Claim it!
- God will do His part, but first we must do our part. He will keep His promise if we obey His commands. Keep in mind that our response to His commands precedes His part in the transaction.
- God wants our total trust. Yes, total. Nothing held back. No games. No empty, pious-sounding words. No, He commands our absolute confidence.
- There is no area which He is unable to handle. Did you note the twice-repeated "all"? God is a specialist in *every* circumstance. That includes yours. Today.
- Since this promise is to be personally applied, how about filling in the blank with your current stress right now? Instead of reading:

. . . in all your ways recognize Him, and He will smooth out your path, removing all obstacles.

you fill in the space:

. . . in _____ recognize Him . . .

Right this moment, take that worry that is eating away at you like a rapidly growing cancer, and turn it over to Him as you write it in that blank space. Refuse to brood over it any longer! Cast aside doubt and fear and leave it *all* with Him. Then stand back and watch Him work.

On the authority of His own Word, I can assure you, He *will* go to work on your behalf. On top of all that, He will "loosen your strings" so your bow won't break.

SPREADING OUT THE WORK LOAD

There is another side of stress that is easily overlooked, and that is trying to do too much ourselves. All of us have a limit. If those huge freight trucks on the highway have a load limit, you can be sure each one of us does, too. When we try to do more than we were designed to do, our level of anxiety immediately begins to rise. This is a common problem among strong natural leaders who assume too much responsibility rather than delegate the tasks to others who could help shoulder the load. When we don't do that, the bow stays bent and occasionally snaps. Even Christians can crack up!

Moses: An Overworked Servant-Leader

Moses is an example of one who fell into this very trap. He was surrounded by an endless number of needs, people's demands, requests for decisions, and problems to solve. On one occasion, his father-in-law, Jethro, paid him a visit and witnessed the load Moses was living under. Exodus 18 tells the story:

> *And it came about the next day that Moses sat to judge the people, and the people stood about Moses from the morning until the evening. Now when Moses' father-in-law saw all that he was doing for the people, he said, "What is this thing that you are doing for the people? Why do you alone sit as judge and all the people stand about you from morning until evening?" And Moses said to his father-in-law, "Because the people come to me to inquire of God. When they have a dispute, it comes to me, and I judge between a man and his neighbor, and make known the statutes of God and His laws." And Moses' father-in-law said to him, "The thing that you are doing is not good. You will surely wear out, both yourself and these people who*

are with you, for the task is too heavy for you; you cannot do it alone" (vv. 13–18).

The classic account of an ancient workaholic! This wise father-in-law comes right out and faces Moses with the truth: "It isn't good . . . you'll wear yourself out." Jethro saw the whole thing objectively. He saw his son-in-law on the raw edge of exhaustion. The anxiety brought on by that much work would soon take a toll on Moses. He couldn't continue doing it all alone.

Before we proceed, let me ask you: Does this sound like your biography? Are you the type who tends to take on too much . . . to handle the demands all alone . . . to hang in there without much thought of passing the load around? To quote Jethro's counsel, "The thing that you are doing is not good." Perhaps this is the bottom-line reason you've become so anxious in recent days. Be honest enough to admit it if it's true. That's the first (and most important) step in the process of change.

As Moses listened, Jethro continued:

Now listen to me: I shall give you counsel, and God be with you. You be the people's representative before God, and you bring the disputes to God, then teach them the statutes and the laws, and make known to them the way in which they are to walk, and the work they are to do. Furthermore, you shall select out of all the people able men who fear God, men of truth, those who hate dishonest gain; and you shall place these over them, as leaders of thousands, of hundreds, of fifties and of tens. And let them judge the people at all times; and let it be that every major dispute they will bring to you, but every minor dispute they themselves will judge. So it will be easier for you, and they will bear the burden with you. If you do this thing and God so commands you, then you will be able to endure, and all these people also will go to their place in peace.

So Moses listened to his father-in-law, and did all that he had said (vv. 19–24).

Moses was smart to listen. He was hearing the advice of a wise man.

Now don't misunderstand. The plan was not that he should back out of the scene completely. No, that wouldn't have been best. His presence was still extremely valuable. But he was to determine those things he should handle—the really weighty issues—then pass around to qualified people the balance of the workload.

Did you notice that those who were to help him needed to be well qualified? Read again the specifics in verse 21:

- Able men who fear God
- Men of truth
- Those who hate dishonest gain
- Leader types

Had Moses chosen the wrong kind of delegates to help handle the work load, his stress would have *increased*, not decreased.

He did as Jethro had suggested:

> *And Moses chose able men out of all Israel, and made them heads over the people, leaders of thousands, of hundreds, of fifties and of tens. And they judged the people at all times; the difficult dispute they would bring to Moses, but every minor dispute they themselves would judge (vv. 25–26).*

This, no doubt, enabled him to have many more effective years of meaningful leadership. We would do well to follow his example.

But What about You?

The real issue, however, is not the anxiety of Moses. It is you and your stress fractures. What is it that makes you think you are capable enough to handle more than you should? Why do you feel the need to continue living under the heavy weight of anxiety when it seems so natural to spread the work among several others?

I challenge you: Release your grip on all those details! Find a few qualified people to help you get the job done. This same principle works when you are under the pressure of an intense trial in your life. No need to tough it out alone. Share it. Let a few people enter into that lonely experience with you. They can stand by you and provide an enormous amount of support, relieving much of the stress you would otherwise be enduring alone.

SHIFTING THE STRESS BY PRAYER

Prayer is another relief—an *essential* therapy during stressful times. I'm reminded of David on one occasion. He and a group of his men returned home after a weary three-day journey. They found that while they were away, an enemy tribe had made a raid on their homes and had burned them to the ground. On top of that, their wives and children had been taken captive by the enemy. It wasn't very long before their morale hit bottom.

> *Then David and the people who were with him lifted their voices and wept until there was no strength in them to weep (1 Samuel 30:4).*

What stress! To make matters even worse, mutiny broke out. The men spoke of stoning David because they were embittered against him. They indirectly blamed their leader for what was happening (that still goes on, by the way). We read of David's response:

> *Moreover David was greatly distressed because the people spoke of stoning him, for all the people were embittered, each one because of his sons and his daughters. But David strengthened himself in the LORD his God (v. 6).*

In the depth of discouragement and the height of stress, "David strengthened himself in the LORD his God." He got alone and prayed. He shifted the pressure from his own shoulders to Jehovah's. He knew that the stress was too big a load for him to carry alone, so he "trusted in the Lord with all his heart," and God immediately began to push away the obstacles.

ENTERING INTO REST

We've thought about overcoming worry by leaning totally and consistently on the Lord, refusing to rely on our own strength and ingenuity. We've talked about delegating your work loads that produce anxiety. We've also considered the value of prayer; simply calling on God for relief and wisdom. These are essential techniques in keeping ourselves out from under the weight of anxiety.

But there is one more scriptural insight on stress that isn't mentioned very often. It has to do with cultivating a lifestyle characterized by rest—a mental and emotional rest, virtually free of the tyranny of the urgent.

The biblical basis of this inner rest is found in Hebrews 4, a chapter that has its roots in the Old Testament:

> *Therefore, let us fear lest, while a promise remains of entering His rest, any one of you should seem to have come short of it. For indeed we have had good news preached to us, just as they also; but the word they heard did not profit them, because it was not united by faith in those who heard. For we who have believed enter that rest . . . (vv. 1–3a).*

The Rest Available Today

The Hebrew people, to whom these words were originally addressed, understood that the writer had their forefathers in mind . . . those people who came out of Egyptian captivity under Moses' leadership. And what does he say of them? Look back at the verses you just read. The truth they heard "did not profit them." Why? Because it remained merely truth—sterile, theological, unrelated information—unmixed with their faith. They heard about God's provisions, they heard about how He would give them the Promised Land, but they didn't take all of it personally. His truth and their faith remained two distinct and separate factors. They failed to enter into the rest He made available. They continued to operate on the basis of sight, which led them into fear, then stress, and finally open unbelief.

Does that mean there's no more "rest" available for God's people today? Quite the contrary.

> *There remains therefore a Sabbath rest for the people of God. For the one who has entered His rest has himself also rested from his works, as God did from His. Let us therefore be*

*diligent to enter that rest, lest anyone fall through following
the same example of disobedience (Hebrews 4:9–11).*

God continues to hold out to all His children a peaceful,
worry-free lifestyle that we can enter into on a moment-by-
moment basis.

Will it happen automatically? No, we are instructed to "be
diligent to enter that rest." What does that mean? Simply this:

1. We acknowledge that our God is in full control of our
lives. No accidents or surprises occur. He calls the shots.

2. We take Him at His Word. We believe His promises (the
Bible is full of them—by the *hundreds*).

3. We claim them by faith. We apply them to our particular
circumstance almost as if God were speaking directly to us this very
moment.

4. We rest in Him. We consciously refuse to worry or fret
over how He is going to work things out. By entering into that
rest, we cease from our own works just as deliberately as our
Creator-God ceased from His works on the seventh day of the creative week.

5. We continue in that calm frame of mind until God sover-
eignly intervenes and solves the problem. We keep trusting in Him
with all our hearts. And every time an alien thought of anxiety flits
through our minds, we turn it over to the Lord in prayer.

This is perhaps the best way to explain one of my favorite
verses, Psalm 46:10:

Cease striving and know that I am God.

The marginal reference suggests the alternative rendering, "Let
go, relax." What a beautiful, refreshing thing it would be to see
most of God's people *relaxing* in Him! Really, thoroughly at peace
as we lean on Him.

Again: What about You?

When are you going to do this, my friend?

That's the key question. What's it going to take to make you
"let go, relax"? He is your Lord, longing to take the burden and

carry it for you; but He won't force you to let go. You must do that yourself. You must take the risk and, in faith, entrust it all into His care. He says to you, "Then, and only then, will you know that I am God."

It's like the familiar yet descriptive story of the tightrope walker who stretched his cable across the vast expanse of Niagara Falls. He walked across and back with his balancing pole as the mist of the falls sprayed all around him. Next he walked across and back without the aid of his pole. Everyone burst into loud applause. His next trip was with a wheelbarrow. To the amazement and delight of the crowd, he went all the way across, pushing the clumsy wheelbarrow with no difficulty at all.

A wide-eyed little five-year-old boy was standing near the acrobat. Suddenly, the man looked right at the boy, smiled, and said: "Son, I'm going to push this wheelbarrow back across the rope. Do you believe I can do it?"

"Yes, sir. I sure do!"

"You mean to say you have that kind of faith in me? You really believe I can do it?"

"Yeah, I really do!"

"Okay, son, get in the wheelbarrow."

That's another story entirely, isn't it? But not until we "get in" do we really entrust ourselves to God's care. Not until then do we "cease striving" and enter into His rest.

The removal of stress is not automatic. It is the cooperative effort of the Christian and his God. May our God be allowed entrance into your mind and be given the reins of your life so completely that all your stress is replaced with peace, as all your fear is removed by faith.

———

God of peace, we long to be more like You in our everyday life. But we are so different.

You are calm and patient; we are often in a hurry, irritable.

You are free from worry; we are frequently in its grip.

You are stable, reliable and gracious; we ricochet from peace to panic.

You are infinitely wise, always right; we wrestle daily with the plague of imperfection.

But we are Your children, valuable to You because we are in Your Son, Jesus Christ. We thank You for not pushing us away when we have failed and fallen. We are also grateful that You deal with us in grace when we run ahead instead of wait, when we doubt instead of trust. You are kind and forgiving . . . and we love You for it!

Take away the things that rob our peace—the things we have confessed to You as we read this chapter. In their place, give us renewed hope and a fresh beginning. Please, Father, do that now.

We ask these things in simple yet sincere faith,
Amen.

CHAPTER TWO

PEACE . . .
IN SPITE OF PANIC

Honestly now, which virtue brings you the most satisfaction, the greatest relief, the deepest sense of comfort and reassurance?

It's peace, isn't it? It's that tranquility of soul that frees you from fear and takes the sharp edges off your anxiety.

Peace is more than an international pursuit. More than an absence of warfare between opposing forces. The kind of peace we'll be looking at in this chapter is inward peace, personal peace, a strong, rock-like confidence that things are not running wild. The Hebrew term is shalom. It can be loosely defined as the deliberate adjustment of one's life to the will of God. Or, as one of the ancient prophets put it, it's trust in action.

> *The steadfast of mind Thou wilt keep in perfect peace,*
> *because he trusts in Thee. Trust in the LORD forever, for in God*
> *the LORD, we have an everlasting Rock (Isaiah 26:3–4).*

Indeed we do! And it's been my observation that apart from the Rock, peace is merely a distant dream . . . a political football to be kicked back and forth by eloquent ambassadors . . . a philosophical fantasy . . . that glorious moment in history when everybody stands around reloading!

So let me assure you before you turn another page, the peace of which I write is inseparably connected to the only One who can provide

31

the inner calm in which peace can survive.

In spite of panic bursting like bombshells all around us, the peace that God can give is there for us to claim like a shelter in a storm, like an anchor of hope when all seems hopeless. Like . . . well, like a rock. Solid, sound, and eternally secure. Read on, and you'll see what I mean.

⸻

I invite you to focus your full attention on one of the rarest of all virtues. It is a virtue that everybody pursues, but very few possess on a regular basis. I'm referring to the often-longed-for but seldom-found virtue of peace.

Peace—something that is needed between nations just as badly as it is needed between neighbors. I was surprised to read one authority who said that in a total of 3,530 years of recorded civilization, only 286 of those years have been spent without war taking place on this globe. During that same period of time, eight thousand peace treaties were broken.[1]

We are a warring people. Deep down underneath our placid plastic cover we are *fighters*. I say this in spite of the fact that a plaque near the United Nations building reads, "They shall beat their swords into plowshares and their spears into pruning hooks; nation shall not lift up sword against nation, neither shall they learn war any more." And even though a portion of the United Nations charter reads, "Our purpose is to maintain international peace and security and to that end: to take effective, collective measures for the prevention and removal of threats to the peace."

If the failure to bring peace to all nations weren't so tragic, the whole idea would be hilarious. One wag was far more serious than humorous when he said, "Washington has a large assortment of peace monuments. We build one after every war."

What's true on a global level is, of course, true of individuals. Most people don't live at peace with themselves, so it stands to reason we don't live peacefully with others. We are basically critical and intolerant. We are in an endless wrestling match with insecurity, a lack of confidence, a struggle with a purpose and place in life, and the pursuit of freedom from worry and anxiety. That's true among Christians as well as non-Christians. How very few live a life that is calm, deliberate, free from anxiety.

Well, you say, that's fine if you're passive by nature, but if you're a leader, then you simply have to worry a lot. Especially strong natural leaders! You have to be involved in the whole tiring process of getting people motivated. And that certainly leads to anxiety.

No. As a matter of fact, it shouldn't. Frank Goble, in his book *Excellence in Leadership*, includes a particular chart that is of interest to me. It's a chart on psychological maturity among leaders on one side, and then on the other side he lists the immature characteristics. Among the thirty-four characteristics contrasted, four read as follows: "The immature leader is critical, emotional, tense, and impulsive. The mature leader is tolerant, calm, relaxed, and patient."

Even an authority in the field of leadership admits it takes peace to be a good leader.

PEACE ACCORDING TO A PROPHET NAMED ISAIAH

Tucked away in the twenty-sixth chapter of Isaiah are two verses we need to dust off every once in a while. I'd like to do that right now, even before we observe and examine an exemplary model—the apostle Paul, a strong natural leader who lived at peace with himself and with others. I want us to see from the prophet Isaiah (who lived eight hundred years before Paul's day) some basic principles about peace itself.

I'd like you to take note not only of what these verses are saying, but also of what they mean to you personally. I want to draw my remarks from the colorful Hebrew language, which is the original text of Isaiah 26:3–4. Remember, the prophet is not writing about international peace. He's talking about an individual at peace with himself, with God, and with others. Let's take a closer look at those two verses.

> *The steadfast of mind Thou wilt keep in perfect peace, because he trusts in Thee. Trust in the LORD forever, for in God the LORD, we have an everlasting Rock (Isaiah 26:3–4).*

Steadfast is from a term that means "to lean, to rest, to support." It's the idea of being sustained as a result of leaning on something supporting you. The words "of mind" come from one verb that means "to frame" or "to fashion, to form." In the original Hebrew language, this particular construction has the idea of "a frame of mind."

If you put the two thoughts together, they convey this: "A frame of mind that is receiving support from leaning and therefore is being sustained." That brings us to the main verb, *wilt keep*. The term means "to guard from danger, to *watch over*." It is so rendered in Isaiah 42:6.

The frame of mind that is being supported as a result of leaning: Thou, Lord, will watch over with "shalom, shalom." Not literally "perfect peace," but "peace, peace." In the Hebrew, a term was repeated for emphasis. So here the idea is of an unending security, a sense of uninterrupted, perpetual rest and calmness. It doesn't come from some human being. According to the prophet's words, it comes from the God upon whom the person leans.

How does God know when to give us that rest? Well, it says in verse 3, *because we trust in Him.* In the Arabic (occasionally closely related to the Hebrew), the term for *trust* has a very picturesque meaning: "to throw one's self down upon one's face."

I think of a trampoline when I think of that imagery. I think of jumping up and down and letting all of my weight fall in an almost relaxed manner on a trampoline. You can just feel yourself bouncing off that stretched-out piece of thick vinyl.

The thought here is that you abandon all other crutches you could lean on, and place all of your anxiety, all of your being, and all of your circumstances on the only One who can support you.

Can He support? Good question. Read on . . . it says that He is an *everlasting Rock.* Now it would hurt us to fall on a large, solid rock. But it's not the idea of falling you must remember. It's the idea of *leaning.* It's the thought of leaning on something that will be perpetually supportive, solid enough to sustain your weight.

Putting all the above together, the paraphrase would read like this: "A frame of mind that is receiving support from leaning and, therefore, is being sustained, Thou, Lord, will watch over with infinite calm. Because he leans fully and relies upon You and none other, You, Lord God, are the everlasting support."

This is the scene of a tranquil, restful mind in spite of circumstances. What a marvelous, limitless promise!

I recently came across Isaiah 26:3 and 4, and am I glad I did! It's been a sustaining force and source of strength in my own life, particularly during a recent week I endured. What a week! I hardly know how to describe it. There won't be another like it. (Hear that, Lord?) Maybe I should pray, *Let there be no other!* There were disappointments. There were jolts. There were surprises. There were family illnesses. There were constant demands.

But behind the scenes . . . there was a great measure of peace in my heart. Yes, there were times when I became anxious. Three or four times I was *really* anxious, but for the most part, when I claimed the truth and entered into a personal experience of verses 3 and 4, there was a distinct difference. When I said, "Lord, I consciously now lean on You and abandon all of my strength for this situation," He held me up.

This is not merely print from a page in the Bible. This is a biblical principle that works in the trenches of life. It begs to be applied. It reaches out from the page with long arms and stretching hands, saying, "Take me. I'm yours, Christian, please take hold of me. You have to claim me." That's what I want you to do as a result of reading the next few pages.

PEACE ACCORDING TO A PASTOR NAMED PAUL

Let's turn to the New Testament (eight hundred years later in time, but still nineteen-hundred-plus years back from our perspective) and look at Acts 19:21–41.

> *Now after these things were finished, Paul purposed in the spirit to go to Jerusalem after he had passed through Macedonia and Achaia, saying, "After I have been there, I must also see Rome." And having sent into Macedonia two of those who ministered to him, Timothy and Erastus, he himself stayed in Asia for a while.*

And about that time there arose no small disturbance concerning the Way. For a certain man named Demetrius, a silversmith, who made silver shrines of Artemis, was bringing no little business to the craftsmen; these he gathered together with the workmen of similar trades, and said, "Men, you know that our prosperity depends upon this business. And you see and hear that not only in Ephesus, but in almost all of Asia, this Paul has persuaded and turned away a considerable number of people, saying that gods made with hands are no gods at all. And not only is there danger that this trade of ours fall into disrepute, but also that the temple of the great goddess Artemis be regarded as worthless and that she whom all of Asia and the world worship should even be dethroned from her magnificence." And when they heard this and were filled with rage, they began crying out, saying, "Great is Artemis of the Ephesians!"

Now skip down to verse 35:

And after quieting the multitude, the town clerk said, "Men of Ephesus, what man is there after all who does not know that the city of the Ephesians is guardian of the temple of the great Artemis, and of the image which fell down from heaven? Since then these are undeniable facts, you ought to keep calm and to do nothing rash. For you have brought these men here who are neither robbers of temples nor blasphemers of our goddess. So then, if Demetrius and the craftsmen who are with him have a complaint against any man, the courts are in session and proconsuls are available; let them bring charges against one another. But if you want anything beyond this, it shall be settled in the lawful assembly. For indeed we are in danger of being accused of a riot in connection with today's affair, since there is no real cause for it; and in this connection we shall be unable to account for this disorderly gathering." And after saying this he dismissed the assembly.

In these twenty-one verses it is not difficult to pick out three significant moments that normally bring anxiety.

To begin with, Paul is shutting down a very successful ministry. I say "shutting down," but perhaps I should say he is leaving it in order to go on his way to new vistas of ministry. Ephesus has been his "headquarters" for a three-year period of ministry. Verse 21 looks back: *Now after these things were finished . . ."*

When you read that in your Bible, remember there's an invisible arrow that points back up to verses 1 through 20. And remember, you have to integrate verses of Scripture with their historical context, much like a setting of a precious gem is placed in a ring. Every precious verse of Scripture fits into its own unique setting. The setting of verse 21 is what we could call a successful ministry— but not one without problems or difficulties.

> *After these things were finished [he now looks to the future], Paul purposed in the spirit to go to Jerusalem after he had passed through Macedonia and Achaia, saying, "After I have been there, I must also see Rome."*

I must also see Rome! It was a burning goal in the apostle's heart. An obvious characteristic of good leadership is goals and objectives. There are dreams. There are plans. An individual who simply lives from day to day is really not having a purposeful life. But Paul isn't like this. He has a goal and it's clear. He hopes ultimately to reach Rome.

Why Rome? Why is that so significant? Rome was the Oval Office of the world, the place of ultimate clout. The emperor lived there. Saints lived in Caesar's palace. Paul knew that if he could reach Rome, he could reach some of the most influential Christians of the known world. Also, quite probably, he could gain an audience with the emperor himself. He longed to speak to Caesar about Jesus Christ.

PEACE AMIDST UNFULFILLED DREAMS

Some of you who read these words have never shared your deepest dreams or highest goals with anyone . . . but they are there nevertheless. And the tendency is to be frustrated before you reach the ultimate goals and dreams of your life.

Paul, however, was at peace with those dreams. His goal, remember, was "I must see Rome." Now read verse 22:

> *And having sent into Macedonia two of those who min-istered to him, Timothy and Erastus, he himself stayed in Asia for a while.*

If you check several verses of Scripture, you will discover that Paul was in Ephesus three years in all. Chapter 20, verse 31 tells us that. Chapter 19, verse 8 says he began with a three-month ministry in the synagogue. Chapter 19, verse 10 says he later ministered for two years at the school of Tyrannus, so we've got twenty-seven months accounted for. But he was in Ephesus thirty-six months. Meaning what? Meaning that nine of the thirty-six months were spent (verse 22) staying in Asia after he got the dream to go to Rome.

When you have a dream and a purpose and some goals in life that you really want to see occur, your tendency is to leave the immediate and to get on with the goals rather than to stay faithful in the assignments of the present.

With that thought in mind, let me give you the first of three definitions of peace. Here it is: *Peace is the ability to remain faithful in spite of the panic of unfulfilled dreams.*

You and I have goals and dreams and desires that are not yet fulfilled. Our tendency is to mount our race horse and gallop in that direction, leaving the present assignments as we get on with those much more exciting dreams. Peace is the ability to remain faithful—even when those dreams are not being fulfilled. If you forget that, you'll be frustrated and your peace will quickly disappear.

When I entrust my frame of mind to Him and lean on my everlasting Rock, He supports me with the ability to stay at the task as I let Him open the doors of the dream . . . in His time.

Now, some of you need that more than others. (I personally need it a great deal.) When you do lean on Him, you may anticipate things leveling out. As you remain faithful to those less exciting tasks, your life at least should naturally become more calm and easy to handle. Right?

Wrong. As a matter of fact, it's like the old saying: "Cheer up.

Things could be worse. So I cheered up and, sure enough, they got worse!" Paul may have thought, "Well, things are gonna get better. I know that these last few months will just run along rather smoothly and unruffled."

But they didn't. Things just got worse.

Look at the next verse. This is after Paul has been willing to stay at the task with Rome on his heart (verse 23). *"About that time . . ."* That's the way it happens. Just about the time you get out of your prayer closet and you've got it all worked out, everything breaks loose. Look at the rest of verse 23:

There arose no small disturbance concerning the Way [which was a first-century label for Christianity].

About the time you get things settled in your heart and promise, "Lord, I'm not going to panic; I'm going to leave those dreams with You," no small disturbance occurs.

PEACE AMIDST UNPLEASANT CIRCUMSTANCES

What was the problem? Verses 24 and following describe it. First, Paul is publicly accused by a man who doesn't even know him.

For a certain man named Demetrius, a silversmith, who made silver shrines of Artemis, was bringing no little business to the craftsmen; these he gathered together with the workmen of similar trades, and said, "Men, you know that our prosperity depends upon this business."

This was some sort of a century-one trade union. It was a guild of men who worked in the same trade. They worked with silver and built little silver shrines of the temple of Artemis, also called Diana.

The temple of Artemis was the major shrine erected and housed in the city of Ephesus. The Ephesians believed it fell from Jupiter, from the heavens, and landed in the particular location known at that time as Ephesus. And there they built their city around this shrine.

In a way similar to the Muslim pilgrimage to Mecca, many travelers would journey to Ephesus to worship at the shrine of Artemis. This prompted the silversmiths to build the trinkets—the little souvenirs—for tourists to buy. Maybe they hung them around their necks or put 'em on their clothing or stuck 'em on their chariots. Whatever they did with them, the craftsmen made a bundle off the tourists from those tiny silver knickknacks.

One day a craftsman named Demetrius realized their business was taking a turn for the worse. Why? He tells us in verse 26:

> *You see and hear that not only in Ephesus, but in almost all of Asia, this Paul has persuaded and turned away a considerable number of people, saying that gods made with hands are no gods at all.*

You can just hear Paul say that in the school of Tyrannus, can't you?

You see, when you've bought into this lifestyle all of your life, then you have a blind spot, even though you are growing in Christ. This was true of some of these new Ephesian Christians who had been worshiping for years at the shrine of Artemis. But Paul explained to them, "You don't worship there anymore. You worship the one deity, the Lord God of heaven, Jesus Christ Himself."

So they gave up their trinkets and spread the word. Consequently, many other people spread the word as they were won to Christ. Now, perhaps by the thousands, people were leaving the worship of Artemis. There goes the silver trinket market! Suddenly the market for Artemis memorabilia takes a nosedive.

You see, the closer you get to the authentic, the less you care about the artificial. You know the truth, so you don't need little replicas of what is false (to say nothing of what is true). You commit yourself to the living Lord who is not seen, who is not heard (audibly). So who needs little tin gods! Who needs religious souvenirs! When you're serving the God of heaven, who could care less about gods on earth?

So now the craftsmen have it in for the missionary. They're saying, in effect, "It's all Paul's fault. He's to blame." Weird, isn't it? When you declare the truth you're often blamed for it even though you didn't write it. You're just declaring it. But people have no other source to turn to. They can't take a swing at God. So those

who represent the Lord and His truth become the scapegoat . . .
the verbal punching bag. This is the place Paul found himself in.
He didn't make anybody do anything. God changed lives. But he
was the voice box.

Still, look at what happened. Now remember, this is the man
who has said, "Lord, I give You my future. I'm relying on You to
take care of it." Things got worse. Look at the unpleasant circumstances.

> *"And not only is there danger that this trade of ours fall
> into disrepute, but also that the temple of the great goddess
> Artemis be regarded as worthless. . . ." And when they heard
> this and were filled with rage, they began crying out, saying,
> "Great is Artemis of the Ephesians!" (vv. 27–28).*

So they're chanting this great cry like you would chant a
cheer at a ball game. "GREAT IS ARTEMIS OF THE EPH-
ESIANS!" They're screaming it—thousands of them. I say that
because of the next verse:

> *And the city was filled with the confusion, and they
> rushed with one accord into the theater. . . .*

That theater is still standing in Ephesus. It can seat up to
fifty-five thousand people. Let's say it was nearly full—fifty thousand people or more chanting, "Great is Artemis of the Ephesians!"
I'm sure that in the city of Ephesus Paul could hear it.

Eventually the word gets to him, "Your name is being used
over there and are they mad!" In fact, verse 29 says they dragged a
couple of his companions into this place that was normally the
fighting arena for gladiators. Gaius and Aristarchus, Paul's traveling companions, were forced to face this mob that was now
intensely angry—an uncontrollable scene of panic.

What would you do? Frankly, I'd probably take the night
train to Memphis! I'd get out of there, like fast. Not Paul. Paul's at
peace. Look at the next verse. A paraphrase of verse 30 would be,
"Let me at 'em."

And when Paul wanted to go into the assembly [there it is], the disciples would not let him. And also some of the Asiarchs who were friends of his sent to him and repeatedly urged him not to venture into the theater (vv. 30–31).

"Don't go out there, Paul! Man, that's bedlam out there. That's suicide. That's crazy." Yet Paul is ready to walk into the scene.

Why? First of all, he's courageous. He doesn't want Gaius and Aristarchus taking the heat for him. Second, he has peace, which allows a person to experience a degree of invincibility. When you live free of anxiety, there is an "envelope of invincibility" in your spirit. It surrounds you, and you don't sense the intimidation of a mob or the fear of peril. It's nothing short of magnificent.

This brings us to the second definition: *Peace is the ability to stay calm in spite of the panic of unpleasant circumstances.*

Now, in case you choose to live like this and to lean in that manner on the living Lord, I want to warn you ahead of time, *people won't understand.* If you're in a situation that calls for panic, yet you don't panic, they're going to want to know what's wrong with you. Isn't that interesting? Our mind-set is so panic-oriented that when you aren't panicked, you have to explain what's *wrong* with you. Amazing!

Are you facing an uncontrollable situation, an uncertainty? Something you just can't extract happiness out of? A situation that's unpleasant, uncomfortable, and dissatisfying? The Lord wants us to glorify Him and to walk in peace with Him, even though our surroundings are unpleasant.

Do you remember the first Apollo moon launch years ago? The astronauts, of course, were being closely monitored. At the time of lift-off, it was reported that their pulse rate was the same as just before or just after. Can you imagine? Man, if I'd have been in one of those helmets I'd have said, "Wow! Look at that! We're LEAVING! We're going! We're on our way! Look, guys, lean over here. Hey, look at this side." My heart rate would've soared! Not theirs. They probably said, "Well, it is now 10:15. Ho-hum . . . We just left. Wake up, Frank. Frank! Ralph, wake up Frank over there. He's not taking in the sights . . . (snoring sound)."

That's the result of great training. And, spiritually, we can be like those astronauts. That's the whole purpose of having a permanent Rock beneath us. Otherwise, what do we have that the world doesn't have? Anyone can be at peace when everything's pleasant. That's no test. It's when "all hell breaks loose" and we don't have it together and we can't control the situation that the test comes and God is there to say, "You just lean on Me. You don't have the answer? Great! That's right where I wanted you. You can't control it? You can't manipulate it? Marvelous! Just wait! Just relax. You're not happy? You're not singing the hymns? Oh! I can give you hymns to sing that you'd never believe, and I don't even need to change your circumstances."

David often begins his psalms at the bottom of the valley and by the time the song is over he's at the top of the mountain. The amazing thing is that it only took him maybe a day or two to write the psalm. What changed? DAVID CHANGED. His circumstances didn't. And he's singing the hymn at the end of the psalm even though his circumstances are unchanged.

Now Paul isn't panicked. He says, "Look. It's not fair for Gaius and Aristarchus to be out there in the theater. I need to be out there."

"No, no! Don't go out there, Paul! Those people mean what they say." So he's wisely counseled to stay back, but the point is, he's at peace. Perpetual peace. Shalom, shalom.

If you live intimidated by people, then you need to come to terms with your lack of peace. God is bigger than any person. Learn to focus on people through the lens of God's eye, and you'll never see anyone even near His match. No mob is out of His control. You can handle it. As a child of God, greater is He who is in you than all of those people who are in the world.

You don't need to dread tomorrow. You don't need to dread your uncontrollable circumstances. It's a decision that's called "a frame of mind," otherwise known as leaning on the everlasting Rock.

Now there's one more scene where peace stands amidst

panic. We've seen Paul through uncontrollable circumstances. We've also seen him with an unrealized dream. Now we find him facing an uncertain future.

PEACE AMIDST AN UNCERTAIN FUTURE

Things actually got worse.

> *So then, some were shouting one thing and some another, for the assembly was in confusion, and the majority did not know for what cause they had come together (v. 32).*

Can you believe that?

"Why are we here?"

"I dunno. Just keep shouting."

"But what's the purpose?"

"Keep yellin'! Keep yellin'!"

The mob is out there, but they don't even know why they're there. So a guy named Alexander stands up and tries to quiet them down. He makes a defense. Verse 34 tells us this was an anti-Semitic group:

> *But when they recognized that he was a Jew . . . they shouted for about two hours, "Great is Artemis of the Ephesians!"*

A football game lasts about three hours with commercials and halftime, but if you count only the playing time and the huddles between downs, it's about two hours in all. Can you imagine hearing the same chant for the entire playing time of one football game? "Great is Artemis of the Ephesians!" It would drive you mad! And there are fifty thousand or more shouting that same phrase.

Guess who would hear that? Paul! Alexander was unable to quiet them down, and it's uncertain what they're going to do. Not even they know what they're going to do. They're in confusion. So there's increased pressure . . . but observe how God calms them down through an unnamed town clerk (verse 35).

A clerk! Can you believe it? An otherwise insignificant no-name!

> And after quieting the multitude, the town clerk said, "Men of Ephesus, what man is there after all who does not know that the city of the Ephesians is guardian of the temple of the great Artemis, and of the image which fell down from heaven? Since then these are undeniable facts [sounds like a clerk, doesn't it?], you ought to keep calm and to do nothing rash."

I want you to envision this scene. Here's Paul doing that which is right, and here's a group of folks who misunderstand and believe he's doing the wrong thing. They're confused, and at odds with each other. Then out of the blue, a clerk who is responsible for law and order and keeping people on the right track stands to his feet.

He gets his paycheck from Rome, by the way, and he knows that Rome hates riots. He also realizes this city would soon lose its freedom if order didn't return. And nobody save Athens enjoyed their freedom more than Ephesus. So he knows he has to calm them down if only to keep himself on the payroll.

The beautiful part is that he doesn't know Paul and Paul doesn't know him, yet God uses *him* to quiet the multitude. Let's just follow along as he speaks.

> "For you have brought these men here who are neither robbers of temples nor blasphemers of our goddess" (v. 37).

That's true!

> "So then, if Demetrius and the craftsmen who are with him have a complaint against any man [let's do it right], the courts are in session and proconsuls are available; let them bring charges against one another. But if you want anything beyond this, it shall be settled in the lawful assembly."

The reason? Verse 40—Rome is watching!

"For indeed we are in danger of being accused of a riot in connection with today's affair, since there is no real cause for it; and in this connection we shall be unable to account for this disorderly gathering."

"Go home!" Verse 41:

And after saying this he dismissed the assembly.

Who did it? *A clerk.*

While you and I are panicked, not knowing about our tomorrow, God is moving clerks around His board like pawns. You and I can't see His chess board. We don't know the right moves, because we're not God. All we know is our little square, if that! And we cannot move. "It's tough being a rook held in place by a bishop, ya know." We're afraid we'll get picked off. But there is peace as long as God has some pawns.

He never runs out of pawns. He never runs out of clerks. He doesn't need you to pull it off. *He's* doing it. When will we ever learn that? And when will we learn that God cannot lose?

I was so uncertain about my future as an adolescent. I stuttered badly, and didn't think I'd ever be able to give the time of day, much less deliver a speech. But a "town clerk," my high school drama teacher, saw something in me I didn't see. He helped me through speech therapy. I didn't know how to speak in public. But through him, I learned. Eventually, the uncertainty of my future was turned around. Public speaking was an open door I'd never considered as an even remote possibility. High school teachers, pay attention! You can be a "clerk" on God's board.

How about mothers who have kiddos struggling with who they are and where they're going and what they're doing and why they're important? Moms, in those day-to-day, constant assignments you suddenly become God's "town clerk." As such, you take charge of and free your child so that he begins to grow in confidence and can get on his way in life. It happens through the painful, consistent, daily, constant effort of motherhood. Small wonder it's under attack today!

You who hold any position at work, you who work with anyone (and that's everybody, that's all of us), the Lord wants to use us as the "clerk" in somebody else's need for peace. He simply wants us to be available.

Here's the third definition: *Peace is the ability to wait patiently in spite of panic brought on by uncertainty.*

Portrayed here is the panic of getting you from here to there in time. Relax! God knows just the vehicle and He's got the timetable put together so that you can watch Him work.

Just think about the circumstances surrounding the birth of our Lord Jesus. You know the story. When Mary was pregnant and right up toward the end of her pregnancy, she was a resident permanently fixed in Nazareth (several days' journey north of Bethlehem). But the Scriptures said, "It's going to happen in Bethlehem." How do you get Mary to Bethlehem so the baby can be born exactly as God said it? Well, you must move the pawn: Caesar Augustus. Everybody in that day thought, "Ah, how great it is, or how bad it is that Caesar does this or that." Do you know what Caesar was? He was a piece of lint on the prophetic page of Scripture. That's all he was. Nothing more than a pawn in God's powerful hand.

Remember what happened? A census was taken. A couple in Nazareth were forced to return to the place of their roots. So Joseph, being of the tribe of David, left for Bethlehem . . . just in time.

"When the fullness of time came," God moved in. And that's the way it is. That's the way it ALWAYS is.

Lacking the panorama of God's perspective, all we see are the outer limits of our one square. So we panic. "What will I do? How will I handle tomorrow? What about . . . ? What if . . . ? But . . . !"

God says, "Trust Me. Just trust Me. Trust in Me with all your heart and don't lean on your own understanding (remember chapter one?). In all your ways acknowledge Me, and I'll direct your paths."

What does Isaiah say? A frame of mind that is receiving support from leaning and is therefore being sustained, God will keep in "shalom, shalom." Because he casts everything on Him. Everything! And that includes unfulfilled dreams . . . unpleasant circumstances . . . and an uncertain future.

Our Father in heaven, through the increased pressure and the unexpected outcome of our lives, You have a way of reducing our lives to the irreducible minimum. We run out of crutches and it's at that point that You step in and say, "I've been here all the time. Remember, I am the permanent Rock."

Thank You for the timeless message that fell from the pen of Isaiah centuries ago . . . a message that still has a relevant ring to it today. I ask You to bring about a marvelous sense of relief, that release that comes only from leaning on You, Lord God. Heal the stress fracture that was caused by too much panic and not enough peace. Show us again the truth of that gospel song we often sing but seldom model:

> What a fellowship, what a joy divine,
> Leaning on the everlasting arms;
> What a blessedness, what a peace is mine,
> Leaning on the everlasting arms.
>
> Leaning, leaning,
> Safe and secure from all alarms;
> Leaning, leaning,
> Leaning on the everlasting arms.[2]
> I pray in Jesus' Rock-like Name,
> Amen.

CHAPTER THREE

WHEN YOUR COMFORT ZONE GETS THE SQUEEZE

We sent Timothy . . . to strengthen and encourage you as to your faith, so that no man may be disturbed by these afflictions; for you yourselves know that we have been destined for this (1 Thessalonians 3:2,3).

Sometimes we suffer stress fractures because of pain and suffering that have unexpectedly broken through the front door of our lives.

To most people, pain is an enemy . . . nothing more than an invading, adversary force that takes unfair advantage of its victims. Stop and think. Who ever thought of affliction as a friend? How many folks do you know who would encourage you to learn from God's messages, even though they come wrapped in discomfort?

This chapter addresses the subject of adversity from that point of view. It approaches the subject realistically, not mystically. These pages are based on the scriptural suggestion that we are not to be disturbed and demoralized when our comfort zone gets the squeeze. Why? Because during and following those times of distress, our God deposits some of His best lessons into our lives.

So then, as you read what I've written, take time to put yourself in the scene. Think of your own stress fractures, especially those circumstances that seem unusually difficult. Ask the Lord to give you the patience and the perspective to glean much wisdom as you apply what you are reading.

May you grow rather than simply groan through it all!

———◈———

Physician Scott Peck calls it "the road less traveled."

Scholar C. S. Lewis refers to it as "God's megaphone."

Contemporary author Philip Yancey says it is "the gift nobody wants."

English poet Byron referred to it as "the path to truth."

But no one ever said it better than Isaac Watts. While writing the lyrics for a hymn that Christians still sing today, he asked direct and searching questions: "Am I a soldier of the cross, a follower of the Lamb?" And again, "Must I be carried to the skies on flowery beds of ease, while others fought to win the prize and sailed thru bloody seas?"

What is this "road less traveled"? Where is that "path to truth"? I'm referring to pain. It's in pain that God speaks to us through His megaphone. *Suffering* is "the road less traveled." *Affliction* is "the path to truth." *Hardship* and *adversity*—these are the gifts nobody wants. Just the presence of these things in our lives creates tension.

For example, you go to your physician for an annual checkup. He takes an X-ray. Within a few days, he contacts you and says, "We'll need to do a biopsy." After the biopsy, he faces you with that horrible piece of information: You have cancer. There's no getting around it. Enter: high-level tension.

One part of us responds, "I will accept this. There is no such thing as a mistake in the life of the child of God. This is a 'road less traveled,' and I want to travel it carefully and well. I want to learn all that God is saying to me through this affliction."

But another part of us says, "I will fight this to the end, because I am a survivor and because I believe there may well be a cure around the corner. So I will not succumb. I will not lie down in my bed, give up hope, and die an early death."

It is the tension between acceptance and resistance. The conflict is actually a mental struggle between seeing God as a God of sovereign control and viewing Him as a God of gracious mercy. There are lessons to be learned that can only be learned along the road of affliction, hardship, and pain.

SUFFERING IS INEVITABLE

There's no getting around it, pain and suffering are inevitable. Our parents did not escape it, you and I will not escape it, and neither will our children. According to Philippians 1:29, suffering is here to stay.

> *For to you it has been granted for Christ's sake, not only to believe in Him, but also to suffer for His sake.*

There are some today who say, "All suffering is wrong. All who suffer are out of the will of God. If you suffer, you are in sin. And since you are in sin, if you will deal correctly and sufficiently with your sin, your suffering will go away."

That is simply not the truth. Scripture does not support such teaching! To be sure, all suffering is rooted in the fact that sin has entered the human race; however, not only has it been granted that we believe in Christ, but it has also been planned that we suffer.

Second Corinthians 4:7–10 presents a similar set of facts:

> *But we have this treasure in earthen vessels, that the surpassing greatness of the power may be of God and not from ourselves; we are afflicted in every way, but not crushed; perplexed, but not despairing; persecuted, but not forsaken; struck down, but not destroyed; always carrying about in the body the dying of Jesus, that the life of Jesus also may be manifested in our body.*

This represents one of the deep mysteries of God. By *"carrying about in the body the dying of Jesus,"* we enter into the lifestyle of Christ—real living.

A few verses later in 2 Corinthians 4, we read,

> *Therefore we do not lose heart, but though our outer man is decaying, yet our inner man is being renewed day by day (v. 16).*

Again, notice we are decaying. Yet deep within we are being renewed.

First Peter 4:12–13 assures us that suffering should never surprise us:

> *Beloved, do not be surprised at the fiery ordeal among you, which comes upon you for your testing, as though some strange thing were happening to you; but to the degree that you share the sufferings of Christ, keep on rejoicing; so that also at the revelation of His glory, you may rejoice with exultation.*

Look at that, Christian! Are you, right this moment in your life, being reviled? Are you currently under attack as a soldier of the cross? Here's a new way to look at such treatment: You are blessed! Rejoice! It's part of the package. It is inevitable.

> *By no means let any of you suffer as a murderer, or thief, or evildoer, or a troublesome meddler; but if anyone suffers as a Christian, let him not feel ashamed, but in that name let him glorify God (vv. 15–16).*

That's one side of the coin. Suffering is inevitable.

PAIN IS ESSENTIAL

There's another side to this same coin . . . and that's the part that says suffering and pain are also essential. In Psalm 119 there are three verses separated from each other but connected by the same thought—verses 67, 71, and 75.

> *Before I was afflicted I went astray, but now I keep Thy word. . . . It is good for me that I was afflicted, that I may learn Thy statutes. . . . I know, O Lord, that Thy judgments are righteous, and that in faithfulness Thou hast afflicted me.*

A man once told me, "God never had my attention until He laid me on my back. Since then, I've been listening." This strong-willed and stubborn man was fighting back the tears as he spoke those words. And he's only been in the crucible less than two weeks.

Suffering is essential if we hope to become effective for God. A. W. Tozer said it like this: "It is doubtful whether God can bless a man greatly until He has hurt him deeply."[1]

Solomon, in his journal named Ecclesiastes, wrote:

> *Consider the work of God, for who is able to straighten what He has bent? In the day of prosperity be happy, but in the day of adversity consider—God has made the one as well as the other . . . (7:13–14).*

"*Consider.*" In Hebrew, the term means "to inspect." It was used by Moses in Exodus 3, verse 3. When the bush began to burn, he said, in effect, "I will now turn aside and *consider* why the bush is not consumed." It was his way of saying, "I will make an investigation." The term includes the idea of perceiving. When used of oneself, it's the idea of revealing to oneself the truth, examining for the purpose of evaluating.

Let's go back.

> *Consider the work of God, for who is able to straighten what He has bent? In the day of prosperity be happy, but in the day of adversity consider [inspect, examine, gain some objective instruction, slow down and listen]—God has made the one as well as the other. . . .*

Suffering is essential, not only because it softens our spirits, making us sensitive to the voice of God, but also because it reveals our true nature. It shows us the truth about ourselves.

Although this journey along the avenue of affliction is unpleasant and unappealing, it is both inevitable and essential. No one in God's family can remain a stranger to pain and suffering.

AN ANCIENT EXAMPLE

Centuries ago, there was a fine group of Christians in the Macedonian church at Thessalonica. The man responsible for founding that church wrote them a letter of encouragement when he heard of the hard times they were enduring. Even though his missionary travels forced him to press on into other regions, his heart was still moved over their plight . . . so he sent his capable companion, Timothy, to check up on how they were doing.

Unable to get them off his mind, the apostle Paul decided to have his friend travel back to Thessalonica and determine the truth of what he'd been hearing. He wondered how they were doing in the storm of suffering that had followed his departure. He had been concerned about them long enough. It was time for action. The opening statement of 1 Thessalonians 3 reveals his plan:

> *Therefore when we could endure it no longer, we thought it best to be left behind at Athens alone; and we sent Timothy, our brother [to find out how you're doing]* . . .

If one of your kids was studying at a foreign university during a time of great national upheaval and danger, you would understand such concern. You would understand the "therefore" of chapter 3, verse 1.

There's something about being in a context marked by panic, adversity, and violence that gets your attention as a parent. You're uneasy. You don't sleep well. You mentally imagine what your kids might be going through. And you, on occasion, find yourself unable to endure. You *have* to have information about how your son or your daughter is doing.

Exactly what was it Timothy was sent to do? Paul states that he sent Timothy for two reasons: (1) to strengthen the believers and (2) to encourage them as to their faith.

To help you understand the importance of those reasons, let's briefly examine those two terms. The word *strengthen* means "to shore up, to buttress." That's an old word we don't use today— "buttress." One man says, "It's to put a ramrod down one's back to enable him to stand straight and erect, come what may."

"I sent Timothy to put a ramrod down your back, so that you wouldn't slump and shuffle around as though you were being mistreated but would stand tall during the hard times . . . you'd stand erect, like a steer in a blizzard. You'd refuse to bend against the odds. I sent him to add strength to you."

They taught us in the Marines that when you are preparing for combat, you should dig a hole big enough for two. There's nothing quite like fighting a battle all alone. There's something strengthening about having a buddy with you in battle that keeps you from panic. Paul says, "You needed somebody alongside to buttress you, to keep you from surrendering."

Now the second word, *encourage*, is a comforting word. *Parakaleo* is the Greek term. We get the word *paraclete* from it, one of the titles of the Holy Spirit. It's often translated "comfort" in the New Testament, but here it is rendered "encourage." It is the idea of standing alongside another person to put courage into him or her. There is a loving, confident hug of reassurance in the word.

If you've ever gone through the valley, perhaps you could testify that you were able to make it only because a Timothy came to your side. Timothy, in your case, might have been a physician or a counselor or a neighbor or perhaps your own parents. But when the Timothy came, whoever he or she was, it was with a fresh delivery of strength and courage.

Notice, the encouragement had a target—to *"encourage you as to your faith."* Timothy didn't come just to say, "Buck up! You can handle it! Suck it up—that's the way it is in life! Others have made it, and you can too!" He didn't come to be a motivational cheerleader. That's not it. Timothy came to examine and to help strengthen the Thessalonians in their faith.

Let me show you an example of this from the Old Testament, back in 1 Samuel 23. One of my favorite stories, when it comes to relationships, is about Jonathan and David. Young David was hunted by King Saul. Saul was in this crazed state of mind. The paranoid king was convinced that young David was trying to usurp the throne, so Saul forgot all about fighting Philistines and decided his greater need was to fight David, and ultimately to kill him. But in the meantime, Jonathan, Saul's son, had developed a warm and supportive relationship with David, his brother in the faith. Imagine the scene:

> *And David stayed in the wilderness in the strongholds,*
> *and remained in the hill country in the wilderness of Ziph.*

And Saul sought him every day, but God did not deliver him into his hand.

Now David became aware that Saul had come out to seek his life while David was in the wilderness of Ziph at Horesh (vv. 14–15).

You know, it's bad enough to have somebody on your tail, but it's even worse when you *find out* that they are. News reached David in his hiding place: "Saul is out to get you. He's got his army searching for you. They know what you look like. You'd better watch out." Look what happened, according to the next verse:

And Jonathan, Saul's son, arose and went to David at Horesh, and encouraged him in God (v. 16).

You talk about meeting a need! Jonathan became David's single source of earthly support. Stop and imagine how much David treasured that meeting with Jonathan.

We would be amazed if we could find out who the Davids are today. Feeling overwhelmed and pressured, one former pastor's wife in the Northeast wrote: "My husband and I have occasionally felt on the edge of an ill-defined despair. Those were times when we felt a variety of things: a desire to either quit or run, a feeling of anger, the temptation to fight back at someone, the sense of being used or exploited, the weakness of inadequacy, and the reality of loneliness. Such attitudes can easily conspire to reduce the strongest and the most gifted to a state of nothingness."[2] A vivid description of how David surely felt.

Now back to the Thessalonians' situation. They needed a Timothy . . . a century-one Jonathan.

For this reason, when I could endure it no longer, I also sent to find out about your faith . . . (1 Thessalonians 3:5a).

Remember, it wasn't just to "see how they were doing." It wasn't a nosy curiosity. Then, why?

. . . for fear that the tempter might have tempted you, and our labor should be in vain (v. 5b).

That is so practical! One of the great battles within young Christians occurs when the adversary strikes during a time of suffering. The adversary finds that weak link or that chink in the armor, and pushes his way in. That's when our comfort zone *really* gets the squeeze!

"When you can't endure it any longer, you pick up the phone and you call." That's a modern-day paraphrase of verse 5, I guess we can say. "When I could endure it no longer, I sent a friend. I wrote a letter. I took time from my schedule to check up on how you were doing."

We're not isolated islands of solid granite, living out our lives like rocks of Gibraltar. We are eroding grains of sand on the seashore, especially when we are traveling the road of pain. When those age-old waves of affliction are beating against us, we need each other! Timothy's presence must have been a great encouragement to the Thessalonian believers.

Let me add here that on occasion it's wise to trace your churnings. Sometimes you will churn over someone during the night. When you awaken, you'll still be churning over the same individual . . . just can't seem to get the person out of your mind.

This was Paul's situation. *"When I could endure it no longer, I also sent to find out."* Want a little advice for no extra charge? *Don't ignore your churnings.* Trace them. Ask yourself why. Why can't I get so-and-so off my mind? Check up and find out! At the heart of Paul's concern was a *"fear that the tempter might have tempted you, and our labor should be in vain."* Paul didn't want to look back and say, "All of those hours we spent together were spent in vain."

THEOLOGICAL PERSPECTIVE

To keep the right perspective in all of this, we need a solid dose of theology. Back to verses 3 and 4—same chapter, same subject of suffering. Paul has been concerned about the Thessalonians. Look at the theology behind the suffering. He sent Timothy to encourage, to strengthen them, *"so that no man may be disturbed by these afflictions . . ."* (v. 3a).

Before I go any further, I want to analyze that first part of verse 3. Paul states a fact we can rely on. It is this: *Affliction need not unsettle God's people.*

A very interesting Greek term translated *disturbed* is used only here in all of the New Testament. Paul draws it from extra-biblical literature and has inserted it here, under the guidance of the Holy Spirit, to grab the attention of the reader.

Originally, it was used to describe the wagging of a dog's tail. The whole idea was "to be shaken back and forth." The term later grew to mean more than the idea of a dog wagging its tail. Finally, as you come up closer to it, the creature bites! If you are a runner, you know exactly what I'm talking about. Rule number one . . . never trust a dog that wags its tail. Why? It's gonna bite ya! It's going to catch you off guard. AND YOU'RE GOING TO BE DECEIVED! That's the word translated here, "disturbed."

"I don't want you, in the midst of the wagging of all of this experience, to be bitten, shaken, and hurt." A child of God need not be unsettled by affliction.

You know how it happens? It often begins with *questions*. See if these sound familiar: Doesn't God care about me anymore? Isn't He the One who promised to help me? How can He be good and permit this to happen to me? Why doesn't He answer my prayer— is He dead? And then it intensifies into doubt: Maybe I've believed wrongly all my life. These questions cause us to start rethinking our bottom-line convictions. Doubt blights our faith.

Do you know somebody who's struggling through those thoughts right now? You know why they are? They have been deceived by affliction.

Paul realized how subtle the enemy is, so he dispatched Timothy. "I sent him to strengthen and encourage you, so that you wouldn't be full of doubt from these afflictions." That's the idea.

Now there is a logical and practical question we would be wise to ask: How can I keep from being disturbed by affliction? How can I keep from having those doubts that unsettle my faith?

First of all, I remember that I have been destined for this.

> *. . . so that no man may be disturbed by these afflictions;*
> *for you yourselves know that we have been destined for this*
> *(v. 3).*

God, in His sovereign and inscrutable plan, realized that pain had to be a part of our training program, so He destined it for us.

Second, I keep in mind that I have been warned ahead of time. Look at verse 4:

> *For indeed when we were with you, we kept telling you*
> *in advance that we were going to suffer affliction; and so it*
> *came to pass, as you know.*

As I mention warning someone about something important in advance, I recall a familiar scene. I prepared my children for marriage as best I could. And one of my pieces of counsel was this: Falling in love is wonderful. Courtship is great. The wedding ceremony is a memory you'll never forget. The honeymoon is . . . well, it's *pretty good!* But when all of that has taken place and you begin to live the real life, roll up your sleeves and tighten your belt. It's tough. So when they go—not if, but *when* they go—through the difficulties in marriage, they have been forewarned. Both have thanked me, by the way, for the previous "warning."

By being forewarned, we are forearmed to handle the pressures and challenges of married life. It helps to have some advance warning.

It's the same in the Christian life. There's no reason to be scandalized or shocked, because we have been warned ahead of time—unless you were led to Christ and discipled by someone who told you a lie; namely, "trust Christ and all your problems will be solved." Then you are in for a real shocker! But if you have been faithfully and realistically trained, you have been equipped to handle this part of God's training program. You can stand firm through your journey along the avenue of affliction. When your comfort zone gets the squeeze, you're not blown away. You can handle it with remarkable inner peace.

By the way, you can't if you don't have Christ. Without Christ, you can no more enter into this life I'm describing than you can fly by flapping your arms. In order for there to be that ramrod in your back, in order for you to be able to stand firm against times of adversity, Christ must remain in first place.

REACTIONS TO AFFLICTION

When we succumb to those overwhelming feelings of adversity, we tend to have three very normal and human reactions: first, resentment toward a former authority figure; second, isolation from Christian friends; and third, indifference regarding former teaching—we begin to doubt what we were once taught.

Interestingly, all three of those feelings were withstood by the Thessalonians. *"But now . . ."* See the contrast? "I was concerned. I sent Timothy. *But now* Timothy has come back, and he's brought us good news of your faith and love."

Isn't that just like Paul? The man was never petty. He was never nosy. He was sincerely concerned about how they were coming along in their walk with Christ. And he says, "You're doing great." How affirming!

Now note: *". . . and that you always think kindly of us . . ."* (v. 6). You might think, why did he put that in there? Because one of the signs of a twisted response to affliction is resenting a former authority. Guess who gets the business when a Christian in a congregation defects? The defecting Christian will often come back at the teacher. Sometimes it's the pastor. Sometimes it's the one who counseled him or her. But the Thessalonians didn't respond in that way. "I got word that you still love me! You still think kindly of me." So they passed the first test; they weren't resentful of Paul. "I'm encouraged to know that you still think kindly of us. You *always* think kindly of us, so you're doing well. You refuse to blame me for what you're going through."

They also passed the second test . . . remember the second reaction? It's the tendency to isolate oneself from former friends. Look at what he says: "You long to see us, just as we also long to see you."

So often, when people are in a time of distress amidst afflictions, they tend to go to the other side of the street when they see someone familiar approaching. They don't want to answer their phone calls. They don't want to relate to anyone else. They want to be aloof, distant, isolated.

The worst place in the world to be when going through doubts is all alone. You need a friend—someone close, like a Jonathan—to support you. The Thessalonian Christians continued reaching out to Paul. They didn't isolate themselves even though their comfort zone had been invaded. They genuinely desired Paul's encouragement.

Third, they passed the final test as well: They had a firm commitment to spiritual truth.

> *For this reason, brethren, in all our distress and afflic-*
> *tion we were comforted about you through your faith (v. 7).*

There it is again. "We were so encouraged to know you're still believing in prayer, you're still trusting in God, you're still counting on Him to be glorified."

Now don't miss something that Paul quietly drops in toward the end of this paragraph. He says, *"For now we really live, if you stand firm in the Lord"* (v. 8).

Does that surprise anybody else? I would think Paul "had really lived," no matter what. No, that's not true. Nothing helped him stand firm and *really live* like knowing his children in the faith were doing the same . . . in spite of affliction.

PRACTICAL THOUGHTS TO CONSIDER DURING AFFLICTION

I want to point out a couple of things I've been saving until now. These two truths will make all the difference, if you will keep them in mind when assaulted by affliction.

Number one: *As Christians, having our comfort zone invaded is essential . . . not unfair.*

You know a good example of that? The same reason people say, "It's best not to have just one child. It's better to have several in the family." Why? Because when you have brothers or sisters, they invade your comfort zone. They get under your skin. (They also get into your closet!) They have a way of dirtying dishes that you have to clean. They are notorious for messing up a house that you have to vacuum. We who came from large families would agree that it was best—now that we look back. Rather than being unfair, it was essential.

Number two: *As soldiers, suffering hardship in battle is expected . . . not unusual.*

If you lived back in the days of the Second World War as I did, you will remember a phrase that was often repeated: "There's a war on." Remember hearing that? Remember saying that? Someone would ask you about something you were doing that seemed a little extravagant. The person would say, "How can you do that? There's a war on!"

I remember reading the gasoline rationing sticker my dad had stuck on the right corner of the windshield of our car. It had a little statement on it that read, "Is this trip really necessary?" With gasoline rationed as it was, if we were out just taking a drive and it looked like we weren't really going anywhere, someone had the right to say, "Why are you doing that? This trip isn't essential. There's a war on!" Restrictions and warfare go hand in hand. Suffering hardship is par for the course when we're traveling down the avenue of affliction.

Tertullian, in his *Address to Martyrs*, wrote, "No soldier comes to the war surrounded by luxuries, nor goes into action from a comfortable bedroom, but from the makeshift and narrow tent, where every kind of hardness and severity and unpleasantness is to be found." He understood the austerity that accompanies the battle.

I began with a quote from Scott Peck. I want to conclude with another one: "Truth . . . is avoided when it is painful. We can revise our maps only when we have the discipline to overcome that pain. To have such discipline, we must be totally dedicated to truth. That is to say that we must always hold truth . . . to be more important, more vital to our self-interest, than our comfort. Conversely, we must always consider our personal discomfort relatively unimportant and, indeed, even welcome it in the service of the search for truth. . . . [And] what does a life of total dedication to the truth mean?" Dr. Peck lists three essentials: (1) "Continuous, and never-ending stringent self-examination." (2) "Willingness to be personally challenged." (3) "Total honesty." (None of these things comes painlessly!)[3]

God has used every means conceivable—including stress fractures—to get your attention. Perhaps He has not yet gotten it. He will not quit until He does. And He will bring you to a knowledge of the truth, as He invades your comfort zone and escorts you down the road less traveled.

Dear Father in Heaven,

Thank You for being faithful to us in the battle. Thank You for taking away the luxuries of the bedroom and the comforts of the kitchen and the soft, padded carpet of the living room and for pushing us out into the streets. Thank You for the benefits of pain and suffering. Enable us to learn and never forget what You are teaching us; may we, in the truest sense of the word, consider.

May we, from this day forward, resist the temptation to avoid the pain when our comfort zone gets the squeeze. Rather, may we learn from it as we journey down the path of affliction. For Jesus' sake,

Amen.

CHAPTER FOUR

DEALING WITH DEFIANCE

Defiance and stress are inseparable co-conspirators. Together, they scheme to steal your peace of mind.

Although the term defiance does not appear in Scripture, acts and attitudes of defiance often do. No matter what the term, the scene is never pretty.

The same is true in life today . . . but the tragedy is that defiance is frequently permitted and sometimes totally ignored, leaving others in the wake of its serious consequences. Talk about stress fractures!

God never overlooks or winks at defiance. He deals with it, and we are to take our cues from our Lord. This chapter is about dealing with defiance—not only how God does it, but how we are to do it.

May He use these words to help you detect defiance and then strengthen your determination to deal with it.

No one should be surprised that our days are marked by rebellion, stubbornness, arrogance, and defiance. These things were predicted to occur "in the last days" (2 Timothy 3:1–2), and they're right on schedule! The defiance may be as small and hidden as a toddler's temper tantrum or as hideous and treacherous as a terrorist attack in an airport.

Whatever the case, defiance must be counteracted. To yawn and look the other way is never appropriate.

If a person from another planet were to suddenly appear on earth, I think he would be shocked. As he observed our lawless lifestyle, watched the proceedings of a divorce court, read about crime on our streets, felt the pressure and anger from homes, and listened to arguments in school classrooms, he could get the idea that defiance pays off. It would appear that those who break the law and defy authority get away with it.

Homes are often dangerous places to be, permitting rebellion and intimidation. Children are in control. Parents have taken the passive route, yielding authority to their kids. In one particular place a young man sued his parents for parental malpractice, claiming $350,000 in damages. His complaint was that they had inflicted him with "intentional emotional distress." At the time I read of it, the court apparently was falling back in favor of the parents' argument that it was not willful and wanton. They were hoping to win the case, but they weren't sure they would. When I was a little boy, that case never would have made it to court. It would have been seen as contempt for authority instead of "child's rights."

Do you realize that your chance of becoming a victim of crime has doubled in just ten years? Your chance of becoming a victim of a violent crime has increased by more than five times in the same period. Today you have a one in twenty chance of being a victim of any crime. You have a one in one hundred chance of being a victim of a violent offense.

The scene isn't limited to a gang of local thugs. Defiance occurs in the national arena as well. When calamities occur across our land, it is amazing how many people gather, not to give aid, but to steal possessions from helpless victims of the tragedy. I find that unconscionable.

A number of years ago, three tornadoes ripped through Omaha, Nebraska, destroying five hundred homes, damaging one thousand others, killing three people, and injuring over 130 residents. National Guardsmen were called out, not to help in the calamity, but to patrol a thirty-four-hundred-square-block area to prevent looting. The Nebraska governor surveyed the area and said it was the worst case of property damage in the history of Nebraska.

What a sad commentary on our modern society! Military men with weapons were needed to prevent scavengers from helping themselves to victims' belongings in the devastated sections of that Nebraska city.

A COMMENTARY ON DEFIANCE

The best commentary on humanity's defiance is not found in any book, television documentary, magazine, or newspaper. It is found in Scripture . . . God's Book of Truth. Specifically, in the last four verses of Romans 1. These verses peel off all masks, scrape away all the veneer, and get right down to the core of depravity, portraying mankind as

> *being filled with all unrighteousness, wickedness, greed, evil; full of envy, murder, strife, deceit, malice; they are gossips, slanderers, haters of God, insolent, arrogant, boastful, inventors of evil, disobedient to parents, without understanding, untrustworthy, unloving, unmerciful; and, although they know the ordinance of God, that those who practice such things are worthy of death, they not only do the same, but also give hearty approval to those who practice them (vv. 29–32).*

Tough talk, huh? But true, painfully true. And realistic. More honest than an article out of *Time* or *Newsweek*, these verses provide us with an up-to-date commentary on the extent of defiance today.

How does God deal with that kind of stuff? What is His attitude toward rebellion that is *that* blatant? How about when it occurs in the lives of His children? It would be wonderful if we could say defiance is limited to the life of the unbeliever, but that simply isn't the case. As a matter of fact, some of you reading this chapter have to confess that you wrestle with the problem of defiance. Your rebellion has come out in your home. It has begun to affect your work. Even your relationships with people have been hindered because of it. Perhaps your church involvements as well.

Defiance, stubbornness, and rebellion rear their ugly heads in every corner of life.

HOW GOD FEELS ABOUT DEFIANCE

How did God deal with defiance in biblical times? Before we examine the life of one whom God dealt with, let's take a quick look at His attitude, His abhorrence of rebellious acts. Please consider Deuteronomy 21:18–21. Even though this event occurred in the days when the severity of punishment was much greater than today, it nevertheless reveals how strongly the Lord feels about defiance.

I take it, from the way this narrative unfolds, that the person in question is a young man—old enough to live outside the home, but perhaps not quite ready for that. He's living under the roof of his parents, but has been demonstrating insubordinate independence. His lifestyle reveals an unbending determination to have his own way.

> *If any man has a stubborn and rebellious son who will not obey his father or his mother, and when they chastise him, he will not even listen to them, then his father and mother shall seize him, and bring him out to the elders of his city at the gateway of his home town. And they shall say to the elders of his city, "This son of ours is stubborn and rebellious, he will not obey us, he is a glutton and a drunkard." Then all the men of his city shall stone him to death; so you shall remove the evil from your midst, and all Israel shall hear of it and fear.*

I remember the first time I read that passage; I was a teenager! In fact, I was getting pretty big for my britches. I thought about those words till very late in the evening, believe me. I can still remember the chill that ran down my back when I realized how seriously God feels about defiance. I was also grateful that I was not living under the Law! The Lord made no provision for domestic insolence, even when the child living at home was approaching adulthood. Defiance is never excusable, never of little concern.

Before proceeding, perhaps I should clarify that this passage is not suggesting that parents have the right to be despotic dictators in the home, mistreating and manipulating their children. No! Please observe that the parents mentioned in Deuteronomy 21 apparently had attempted to work with their son—to no avail. He defied their authority. He refused to cooperate, to curtail his habit of getting drunk, to restrain himself in other things as well. This young man was turning the home into a "hell on earth." He left the parents with no alternative other than to call on city authorities to help, which still occurs today.

Take time to observe, parents! The peace, the moral standards, and the joy of your home are not to be sacrificed on the altar of indulgence. Defiance will send stress fractures through the structure of a home just as it will ruin a life. If you do not deal with it, who will? Believe me, the teacher at school or the minister at church cannot take the place of the parent at home.

In the days of Samuel, there once lived a self-willed king named Saul. On one occasion King Saul did his own thing, in defiance of God's instructions through the prophet-judge Samuel. The prophet was dispatched by the Lord to face the king. Saul excused himself, backpedaled, rationalized, and even denied being defiant. Finally, Samuel had had enough. He looked straight at Saul, pointed that long, bony finger of his and said, *"Rebellion is as the sin of divination . . . and idolatry."* That's quite a statement! *The Living Bible* captures the thought in this paraphrase:

> *For rebellion is as bad as the sin of witchcraft, and stubbornness is as bad as worshiping idols (1 Samuel 15:23a, TLB).*

The next time you're tempted to pass over defiance, remember that analogy.

AN EXAMPLE OF HOW GOD DEALT WITH DEFIANCE

King Saul may have been rebellious, but King Solomon's story is even more incredible. Although bright, rich, capable, and the son of a famous father, Solomon became an insolent, carnal man. We need to see how God dealt with him—the epitome of defiance.

The part of Solomon's biography that interests us is recorded in 1 Kings 11. This is not a teenaged, rebellious son living under the roof of his parents; this is a middle-aged man who has reached the pinnacle of success. (Remember, there is no age restriction on defiance—you can be defiant and be up in years. You can be defiant as a child, a teenager, or an adult.) By now, Solomon was "running the show" of the kingdom. But, like a bolt out of the blue, he broke free. He must have thought, "I'm going to get my way regardless." He seemed to change overnight. When that happens, it's time for people like us to sit up and learn some lessons. Solomon's life continues to be a warning to all of us.

SEEDS SOLOMON PLANTED

Actually, Solomon's defiance was *not* a sudden thing. Not at all. There were some seeds he'd planted early in life which he later harvested in adulthood.

The first were seeds of *compromise*. Remember when he had an alliance with Pharaoh, and married Pharaoh's daughter? The story is recorded in 1 Kings, chapter 3. As a result of that compromising alliance, he began to make concessions in his spiritual walk. The compromise seeds grew into a loss of distinction as a sensitive man of God. He lost his distinction as a monotheistic Jewish ruler. He had been instructed not to cohabit or even mingle with foreign women. His Jewish upbringing included strong admonitions against intermarrying with Gentiles. The seeds of compromise were now harvested in a loss of distinction.

A little later on in his life, Solomon planted seeds of *extravagance*. He lived extravagantly. He spent extravagantly. He built extravagantly. There were no parameters on his budget. He was able to buy at will, build whatever he desired, and live wherever and however he wished. Self-control and restraint were not in his vocabulary. In the journal he kept, Ecclesiastes, we discover that his fast-lane, go-for-broke lifestyle led to cynicism, boredom, and disillusionment. Such is the fruit of extravagance.

Third, there was *unaccountability*. The more closely you study his managerial habits, the more you realize Solomon was never willing to be accountable—not to any of his counselors, not to any of the prophets, not to any of his wives who surrounded him. We never read of Solomon's asking for straight answers or listening to sound advice. He mentions the wisdom of it—theoretically—in the Book of Proverbs, but it is conspicuously absent in his life. He operated like the Lone Ranger. He was close-minded. Ultimately, he even ignored what God was saying through His spokesmen, which is lethal for any spiritual leader.

The seeds of unaccountability were finally harvested . . . as they always are. The fruit? Unchecked independence. Nobody can get away with unaccountability. After a while, you've got to pay the piper. And that's what Solomon did in the latter years of his life.

One more category of seeds should be mentioned—the seeds of *idolatry*. When harvested, idolatry led to lust and open defiance.

This is precisely where we find Solomon in 1 Kings 11. The man is living in the backwash of carnality. He doesn't know it, but he is about to be dealt with by the Lord God, who always takes a dim view of defiance.

> *Now King Solomon loved many foreign women along with the daughter of Pharaoh: Moabite, Ammonite, Edomite, Sidonian, and Hittite women, from the nations concerning which the Lord had said to the sons of Israel, "You shall not associate with them, neither shall they associate with you, for they will surely turn your heart away after their gods." Solomon held fast to these in love (vv. 1–2).*

Solomon not only married foreign women, he married *many* of them, in direct defiance of Scripture. Defiance always denies Scripture willfully—not ignorantly, *willfully*.

And did you notice how verse 2 closes? *"Solomon held fast to these in love."* He flaunted it. He not only embraced them, he embraced them publicly. He not only married them, he courted them in front of the people of Israel. He not only played around . . . he held fast to them in love.

We should not be surprised to read in the very next verse that *"his wives turned his heart away."* We don't use that expression today. We use the words "turned off." He was "turned off" to spiritual things. The Modern Language Bible says that those women *"perverted his mind."* The foreign women, coming in with their idolatrous and cultural polytheism, brought with them enough seduction to turn him off spiritually. Solomon lived his midlife years turned off to God, which led to old-age open defiance.

> *For it came about when Solomon was old, his wives turned his heart away after other gods; and his heart was not wholly devoted to the LORD his God, as the heart of David his father had been. For Solomon went after Ashtoreth the goddess of the Sidonians and after Milcom the detestable idol of the Ammonites. And Solomon did what was evil in the sight of the LORD, and did not follow the LORD fully, as David his father had done. Then Solomon built a high place for Chemosh the detestable idol of Moab, on the mountain which is east of Jerusalem, and for Molech the detestable idol of the sons of Ammon. Thus also he did for all his foreign wives, who burned incense and sacrificed to their gods (vv. 4–8).*

Solomon's defiance was not hidden; it was out in the open.

Defiance is always a tough thing to deal with. Living with a defiant spouse, however, may be the hardest of all. Some mates are so defiant it takes a harsh argument for the partner to bring to their attention the wrong in their lives. Some children and teens are so defiant that just mentioning their rebellion sets off an incredible explosion in the home. Pastors deal with defiance rather frequently. Sometimes it's a defiant board member . . . or church member . . . or fellow staff member. To be truthful, sometimes it's the pastor who has become a rebel—a defiant, carnal leader. So we're not addressing a problem limited to people in the days of Solomon. Defiance, like taxes, will forever be with us.

HOW GOD RESPONDED

Let's see what God did in response to Solomon's defiance. His very first reaction was *a strong statement of divine anger.*

> *Now the LORD was angry with Solomon because his heart was turned away from the LORD, the God of Israel, who had appeared to him twice, and had commanded him concerning this thing, that he should not go after other gods; but he did not observe what the LORD had commanded. So the LORD said*

*to Solomon, "Because you have done this, and you have not kept
My covenant and My statutes, which I have commanded you,
I will surely tear the kingdom from you, and will give it to
your servant" (vv. 9–11).*

Right off the bat: *"Now the* LORD *was angry with Solomon."* What
a refreshing balance, what a clean breath of air! Of course God was
angry! Week after week we hear of the love of God. We are told of
the compassion and the mercy and the grace of God, and we surely should be. But to the exclusion of His anger? I think not. How
easy to forget that He is holy. How seldom we hear teaching of the
wrath and the anger of God, of the jealousy God has for the purity of His people.

Mark it down in bold print: **Defiance still makes God
angry.**

Not too long ago, I did a scriptural study on divine anger.
To tell you the truth, I was amazed at how often the word *anger*
appears in the Bible in relation to God. Usually, the word *kindled*
accompanies the term. His anger is often kindled. Our English
word has in mind the idea of arousing or stirring something up or
starting embers to glow. It's usually related to the kindling of a fire.
The Hebrew word translated *kindled* comes from the root verb that
suggests "to be heated to the point of vexation." It vexes God when
He sees His children walk against His plan. I repeat, it still makes
Him angry.

I have several old Puritan books. Every time I read them, I
find myself reminded of the holiness of God. God stands ready to
deal with His people, modern-day teaching notwithstanding. We
need the reminder that He is still jealous for our hearts, and when
we walk against His way, He deals with us. The Bible is replete
with illustrations such as these.

Is He patient? Yes. Loving? Of course. Merciful? Always. But
holy? And jealous? Absolutely. Never, ever forget that when we
serve the idols of our own lives, the Lord becomes angry because
our hearts are turned off to Him. Even His longsuffering has a
limit; His patience reaches an end.

It's like what my folks used to say when I finally went too far.

In a tone clearly reserved for finality, they would say: "Charles, THAT'S IT!" Oh—those awful two words! "That's it!" How I would long for a place to hide . . . or the coming of the Lord for His own! At times God says to His children, "That's it! No more!" And He moves right in. Defiance, I find more often than any other attitude, is the thing that kindles God's anger. Let us never forget that our defiance gives Him every right to be angry. We've broken His holy plan for us. He wants us to walk in the light, in fellowship with Him, just as He is in the light.

Did you notice how God said He would remove Solomon's kingdom? According to verse 11, He would *"tear"* the kingdom from him. T-E-A-R. That, my friends, is a serious stress fracture. When we exhibit defiance, forcing the Lord to step in and deal with us, it's a *tearing* experience. It's a ripping away of things that are very important to us. Our peace and calm are disturbed. Our diplomatic relationships with people are stirred up. We don't get along with our parents. We don't get along with our kids. We don't get along with our peers as we once did. All of that is a tearing away of kingdoms that were built in defiance.

Let's not overlook the Lord's mercy here. He says in verses 12 and 13:

> *Nevertheless I will not do it in your days for the sake of your father David, but I will tear it out of the hand of your son. However, I will not tear away all the kingdom, but I will give one tribe to your son for the sake of My servant David and for the sake of Jerusalem which I have chosen.*

Those are hard, strong words. Frankly, defiant people only hear hard, strong words. They are not listening to the whisperings or the quiet movements of God.

Okay, what else does the Lord do? After stating His anger, *He raises up human adversaries.* Look at how He does this—it's intriguing. Get a pencil handy, and look at verse 14 and then verse 23.

> *Then the LORD raised up an adversary to Solomon, Hadad the Edomite; he was of the royal line in Edom (v. 14).*

God also raised up another adversary to him, Rezon the son of
Eliada, who had fled from his lord Hadadezer king of Zobah (v. 23).
Take a moment and underscore two identical phrases. Verse 14:
"The LORD raised up an adversary to Solomon." Verse 23: *"God also
raised up another adversary to him."* The Lord names both adver-
saries: Hadad and Rezon.

Why would I make a point out of these ancient, unknown
names? Trust me, there is a very practical reason. Hadad and Rezon
were two men who had become enemies of David. Perhaps
Solomon didn't even know that fact, since he'd been a little boy
during most of the years of his father's life on the battlefield. He
wasn't even born when his father began to clear the deck and clean
house, making ready for a new kingdom. But Hadad never forgot it.

Look again at verse 14:

> Then the LORD raised up an adversary to Solomon,
> Hadad the Edomite; he was of the royal line in Edom.

So Hadad was a prince on his way to becoming a king in Edom.
The verses that follow fill in all the historical details:

> For it came about, when David was in Edom, and Joab
> the commander of the army had gone up to bury the slain, and
> had struck down every male in Edom (for Joab and all Israel
> stayed there six months, until he had cut off every male in
> Edom), that Hadad fled to Egypt, he and certain Edomites of
> his father's servants with him, while Hadad was a young boy.
> And they arose from Midian and came to Paran; and they took
> men with them from Paran and came to Egypt, to Pharaoh
> king of Egypt, who gave him a house and assigned him food
> and gave him land (vv. 15–18).

Back, years earlier, when David took the throne, the Edomites were
wiped out. Under David's direction, the Israelites slaughtered every
Edomite male except a few who escaped, one of whom was Hadad
of the royal line in Edom. He fled to Egypt as a little boy along
with a few of the servants—no one else got out alive. Hadad
remembered, from those frightening early years, the incredible

slaughter that had accompanied the reign of David. And he never forgot it.

Hadad went to Egypt. He grew up there. In fact, it says in the next two verses:

> *Now Hadad found great favor before Pharaoh, so that he gave him in marriage the sister of his own wife, the sister of Tahpenes the queen. And the sister of Tahpenes bore his son Genubath, whom Tahpenes weaned in Pharaoh's house; and Genubath was in Pharaoh's house among the sons of Pharaoh (vv. 19–20).*

Hadad had married the sister-in-law of the Pharaoh of Egypt. He became quite a man in Egypt. They had a son, and their son played together with Pharaoh's kids in the Egyptian palace. Hadad was very close to the top man in Egypt. But he never forgot David. Never.

Solomon probably knew nothing of Hadad. He was an Edomite, a former king-in-the-making who never made it. He was a forgotten man. But not to God. You see, when the Lord saw the defiance in Solomon's life, He began to whistle for the adversaries, much like you would call the dogs on an attacker. "Hadad, sic him!"

All of a sudden, Hadad got word that David was dead.

> *But when Hadad heard in Egypt that David slept with his fathers, and that Joab the commander of the army was dead, Hadad said to Pharaoh, "Send me away, that I may go to my own country." Then Pharaoh said to him, "But what have you lacked with me, that behold, you are seeking to go to your own country?" And he answered, "Nothing; nevertheless you must surely let me go" (vv. 21–22).*

The writer of this narrative doesn't tell us everything here— just remember Hadad. The way this writer chronicles the story is rather intriguing. He keeps us wondering and waiting. There's another adversary the Lord used to afflict Solomon.

> *God also raised up another adversary to him, Rezon the son of Eliada, who had fled from his lord Hadadezer king of*

Zobah. And he gathered men to himself and became leader of
a marauding band, after David slew them of Zobah; and they
went to Damascus and stayed there, and reigned in Damascus
(vv. 23–24).

The Hebrew says Rezon led "men who killed." The marauding
band was a killing body of men. Rezon is living in Damascus, and
Solomon doesn't know anything about him. Everything is going
well with extravagant Solomon. He's waltzing along the first twenty years of his life, relaxing. All kinds of palaces, storehouses, and
cities are being built. Everything seems to be sailing along smoothly. But erosion is happening. Ever so silently, Solomon turns
against God, knowing nothing about a guy named Hadad or another one named Rezon. Neither of them, however, will ever forget
David and his reign. Finally, both men make their long-awaited
move. Operation revenge!

So [Rezon] was an adversary to Israel all the days of
Solomon, along with the evil that Hadad did; and he abhorred
Israel and reigned over Aram (v. 25).

So there was evil done against Solomon by Hadad. There
was also havoc wrought by another adversary named Rezon. I take
it that from this time on, these guys began to harass and make life
generally miserable for a king who hadn't even known the bad dogs
existed. God unleashed both of them: "Sic 'em, Hadad! Sic' em,
Rezon!"

Talk about practicality! When we have the audacity to defy
the living God, when we walk against His holiness and resist His
authority over our lives, He has ways of calling all kinds of dogs
from any number of alleys. We don't even know they're there, then
boom! He brings them in. Sometimes they come in the form of a
memory . . . it haunts you, it won't leave you alone. It stays there
and plagues you. It stays on top of you. You find yourself restless.
It's like a monkey on your back—it stays, plagues, works, harasses,
beats you black and blue emotionally. Perhaps your sense of defiance gets stronger, and you stiffen your neck and stand your
ground. Guess what? God just calls more of those dogs out of the

alley. "Go get him. Work on him." Just as we saw in chapter 2 that God never runs low on "clerks" or "pawns," He also never runs low on "attack dogs."

He is persistent when dealing with defiance. He will not give relief to His children who deliberately walk away from His will. That includes your children who may have grown up in the Lord but are now running wild. They have their own Rezons and Hadads, trust me. It's just a matter of time before they will surrender.

I memorized a statement by Lord Byron many years ago. I find the content appropriate and penetrating:

> The thorns which I have reap'd are of the tree
> I planted; they have torn me, and I bleed.
> I should have known what fruit would spring from
>   such a seed.[1]

Seeds that one plants grow. Often they bear ugly, treacherous thorns. They grow to such proportions that they bite and sting and hurt and infect us. God uses those thorns to prick us, to get us back on the right path. Why? He's jealous for our lives. He misses the close relationship He once had with us.

There is one more person you should meet. Solomon's other two adversaries brought external oppression. This man brought internal rebellion. Those others lived outside the country—one in Egypt and one in Damascus. Their attacks and skirmishes were from the outside. Not Jeroboam. He was a man whom Solomon trusted.

> *Then Jeroboam the son of Nebat, an Ephraimite of Zeredah, Solomon's servant, whose mother's name was Zeruah, a widow, also rebelled against the king. . . . Now the man Jeroboam was a valiant warrior, and when Solomon saw that the young man was industrious, he appointed him over all the forced labor of the house of Joseph (vv. 26, 28).*

Jeroboam went right on up the ladder. He had all the "moxie," so Solomon promoted him.

The insightful British pastor Alexander Whyte, in his biography on Old Testament characters, gives us a thumb-nail sketch of Jeroboam: "It was amid all the terrible oppression and suffering of that day that Jeroboam rose so fast and so high in Solomon's service. Jeroboam's outstanding talents in public affairs, his skillful management of men, his great industry, and his great loyalty, as was thought, all combined to bring the son of Nebat under Solomon's royal eye, till there was no trust too important, and no promotion too high for young Jeroboam."[2]

Then to crown it all, as time went on, he became the king's personal confidant. Jeroboam was on his way to the top of the kingdom ladder. Why? He'd won the heart of the king. Then, smack-dab in the middle of this promotion, wham! He turned and rebelled against Solomon. Did you catch that in verse 26? *"[He] rebelled against the king."*

The word *rebelled* comes from a root verb in Hebrew that means "to lift one's hand against." Perhaps he physically fought with Solomon in addition to the misery that he brought the king. What an adversary! He did an "inside job" on Solomon.

So Solomon, who months earlier had known only relaxation and extravagance to the point of boredom, is now faced with pit bulls like Hadad and Rezon, as well as a sleek Doberman, Jeroboam, biting and snarling and fighting with him, the king.

There is a proverb that aptly describes Solomon's woe. "The way of the treacherous is hard" (Proverbs 13:15b). You can't defy the living Lord without having misery move in alongside.

David writes in Psalm 32: "For day and night Thy hand was heavy upon me; my vitality was drained away as with the fever heat of summer" (v. 4).

The Lord's hounds are a lot more effective than the FBI's finest. He always gets His man—or woman. Always! He knows where we are all the time. He won't give up.

Living in a tough situation at home right now? Having difficulty with defiance among those who work under you or serve over you? The Lord has never met His match. He is never intimidated by defiance. He just moves so slowly sometimes, doesn't He? Don't you wish He'd get on His horse and ride faster? "Come on,

Lord, how long is this gonna take?" I understand. I've asked the same question.

Verse 40 of 1 Kings 11 says: "Solomon sought therefore to put Jeroboam to death; but Jeroboam arose and fled to Egypt to Shishak king of Egypt, and he was in Egypt until the death of Solomon."

As if the presence of adversaries weren't bad enough, he also encounters *personal frustration*. I mean, here's the king. Surely he ought to be able to kill anybody in the land. He's even got an army available. But here's a guy who escapes! Solomon is so frustrated—he can't even put a hit man on Jeroboam and finish him off. It's as if his hands are tied. So it is when you're in defiance; things refuse to work out. Try all you like, you cannot find relief in wrongdoing.

THE DOWNWARD SPIRAL OF DEFIANCE

Talk about going from bad to worse. Defiance is the classic illustration. First, *defiance begins with carnal attitudes*. Long before there are carnal actions, there are carnal attitudes. It can happen to adults just as quickly as it can to teens or kids. Perhaps it would help if I spelled out a few of the attitudes by describing some actual thoughts in the minds of the defiant.

The first thought says: "I want my own way." Those who are defiant aren't interested in your way, or God's way. "I want *my* way." That is an attitude of *selfishness*.

The second thought says this: "I won't quit until I get it." That is an attitude of *stubbornness*. "I want my way, and I want it when I want it. I will not quit until I get it." That's just plain obstinance; that's stubbornness.

Third: "I don't care who it hurts." In other words, "I want my way. I won't quit until I get it, and I don't care who it hurts—husband, wife, peers, parents, kids, the team, my church—I don't care. I'm gonna get my way." That is an attitude of *indifference*.

Fourth: "I refuse to listen to counsel." Obviously, that is an attitude of *resistance*. "I know God has something to tell me, but I don't want to hear what He's got to say." Or, "I know what He's going to tell me—I know what that Book says. I don't want to listen to God's counsel." That's resistance.

Fifth, and finally: "I am not concerned about the consequences." That's *contempt.* Pushed to the wall, this extreme reaction includes ignoring the consequences—a total lack of concern for the results.

"I want my own way. I won't quit until I get it. I don't care who it hurts. I will not listen to counsel. I am not concerned about the consequences." Those are the words of a defiant person. And they can come from our lips just as readily as from a person without Christ. They represent selfishness and stubbornness and indifference and resistance and contempt. As I mentioned earlier, defiance begins with carnal attitudes.

Continuing the downward spiral, the second inescapable reality about defiance is this: *Defiance leads to personal misery.* Remember Hadad, Rezon, and Jeroboam? They dealt Solomon untold misery. The defiant person wants freedom, but he finds himself captured. He wants his own way, but he finds himself ensnared by the restrictions that misery brings.

Look at Proverbs 13:15 and you'll see a pretty good illustration or statement of that kind of misery. I referred to it earlier but now want to examine two particular terms:

> *Good understanding produces favor, but the way of the treacherous is hard.*

The word *treacherous* is translated from the Hebrew verb that means "to deal treacherously or defiantly." The way of one who deals in defiance is *hard.* Interesting term. It means "to be perpetual, steady, constant, ever enduring, rugged." The etymology of the term finally leads to "ruggedness." The way of the person who deals in defiant thoughts and actions is perpetually rugged, hard, and miserable. Not only Solomon's life but a proverb from Scripture assures us that defiance leads to personal misery.

There is a third stage on this downward spiral: *Defiance results in inescapable bondage.* Those most defiant are most bound, not free.

> *For the ways of a man are before the eyes of the LORD, and He watches all his paths (Proverbs 5:21).*

That's quite a thought. But the next two verses complete the picture:

> *His own iniquities will capture the wicked, and he will*
> *be held with the cords of his sin. He will die for lack of instruc-*
> *tion, and in the greatness of his folly he will go astray.*

Look at that! The "cords" from one's own defiance will wrap them-selves around the victim and will cause him or her to be inescapably bound up. In the margin of my mind I have written "Samson," who was literally bound with the cords of his own sin—unconquered lust.

Frankly, I'm much more concerned about "acceptable" defi-ance than bold defiance. Why? Because that's what happens more often than not. We cover up. We hide our defiance. We sit on the lid. But, sure enough—given sufficient pressure—something even-tually snaps.

Your defiance will come out in the most amazing ways: a bat-tered child; a crime of passion; a blistering tongue-lashing; run-ning away from home; an illicit pregnancy; an ugly, caustic line of profane words; an affair; domestic disharmony; a ruined testimo-ny. I charge you before God to deal severely with this giant. It may be slumbering right now—but I warn you—not for long.

Now that you have reached the end of this chapter, I would like you to think about your life for just a few moments. I'd like you to trace your actions and attitudes back a day or two, or maybe several weeks. Take a long, straightforward look at where you are. Are any signs of defiance there? "I want my own way. I won't quit till I get it. I don't care who it hurts. I refuse to listen to counsel. I'm not concerned about consequences."

My friend, those are dangerous words. If they are there in your head, you're on a powder keg that's going to explode. Your stress fracture will soon become a compound fracture. I ask you to find the hope of forgiveness in Jesus Christ. He is there, and He awaits your turning all that turmoil over to Him . . . that hot caul-dron of resentment. The longer it boils, the more lethal it could become.

Don't rationalize and say, "Well, that's just the way I am."

Call it what it is and say, "Lord, I come to You in my need. I need You to take it, take it now."

———◦———

I ask, Heavenly Father, that in a very personal and wonderful way You will bring cleansing and hope. Some who read this chapter are Your children. Some are not. I pray for both groups. Defiance is such an aggressive enemy! Replace our selfishness, our stubbornness, our indifference, our resistance, our contempt . . . with forgiveness. Release us from the bondage of our sin, dear God.

I invite You to take a walk down the galleries of our minds and lift those pictures off the wall that have no business being there. And flood us with Your forgiveness, Father. Take away all the sting from the long-standing thorns that we're living with. Do this now, Father.

In the name of Jesus I pray,
Amen.

CHAPTER FIVE

MORAL PURITY

Many of us find ourselves stressed to the breaking point as we endure a two-sided battle: On one front, we must cope with a rapidly declining culture—a society racing into a foundationless moral chaos. On a deeply personal level, we find ourselves wrestling daily with a menacing, unrelenting adversary called "Lust."

The following two chapters offer a battle plan for fighting each of these conflicts in turn.

I am well aware of the numerous written materials available today on the subject of moral purity. But I am even more aware of the enormous propaganda to which we are exposed. Our minds and our emotions are easily lured off target by what I often call "the system." By that I mean the endless, relentless bombardment from the world in which we live. Its messages are subtle and bold, written and spoken, always attractive, remarkably convincing, and clever indeed.

Realizing the effectiveness of this sensual network, I am of the opinion that there needs to be a continual stream of information that counteracts this force, presenting scriptural truth in an equally convincing manner. Erroneous thinking that leads to evil actions needs to be confronted. Because "the system" operates twenty-four hours a day, seven days every week, it's doubtful that Christians have come anywhere near overstating their position. With determination and diligence, we must continue to make known a perspective that exposes "the system" and penetrates the moral fog which envelopes all who live on this planet. Hence, the following two chapters.

Although brief, they are forthright. Other works may be more thorough, but none are written with greater passion or deeper conviction. As a pastor since the early 1960s, I have observed a tragic decline—a lowering of the standard of moral excellence—even within Christian circles. What was once confined to "the system" has now invaded the Church. That fact alone is enough to justify an increase in our effort to publish materials that both uphold the need for personal holiness and declare the consequences of an immoral lifestyle.

If something I have written helps you to walk away from wrong that has held you in bondage and draws you back to the truth that will set you free, the purpose of these chapters will have been achieved.

———◆———

Holiness sounds scary.

It needn't be, but to the average American, it is. Our tendency is to think that holiness would never find its way into the office of a salesperson. It would certainly never enter the considerations of an aggressive and successful athletics coach . . . nor a mother of small children . . . a teenager involved in a busy high school . . . nor some collegian pursuing a career with his or her eyes on great financial goals. Let's face it, holiness is something for the cloistered halls of a monastery. It needs organ music, long prayers, and religious-sounding chants. It hardly seems appropriate for those in the real world of the twentieth century. Author John White seems to agree with that:

> Have you ever gone fishing in a polluted river and hauled out an old shoe, a tea kettle, or a rusty can? I get a similar sort of catch if I cast as a bait the word *holiness* into the murky depths of my mind. To my dismay I come up with such associations as:
>
>> thinness
>> hollow-eyed gauntness
>> beards
>> sandals
>> long robes

stone cells
no sex
no jokes
hair shirts
frequent cold baths
fasting
hours of prayer
wild rocky deserts
getting up at 4 A.M.
clean fingernails
stained glass
self-humiliation.[1]

Is that the mental picture you have when you think of holiness? Most do. It's almost as though holiness is the private preserve of an austere group of monks, missionaries, mystics, and martyrs. But nothing could be further from the truth.

As a matter of fact, holiness does belong in the life of the teenager. Holiness does have a place in the office of the salesperson. It is, indeed, appropriate in the world of the up-to-date, aggressive, even successful individual.

I couldn't be in greater agreement with Chuck Colson's statement: "Holiness is the everyday business of every Christian. It evidences itself in the decisions we make and the things we do, hour by hour, day by day."[2]

THE FOG: AN ANALYSIS OF TODAY'S MORAL SCENE

Before going any further, let's back off a few feet and get a little perspective on the moral scene today. To penetrate the fog will take some effort, I can assure you. Perhaps it will help to read the writings of a sixth-century B.C. prophet named Habakkuk. His name looks like a misprint, doesn't it? On the contrary, the man was a bold voice for holiness in a day of compromise. A misfit, perhaps, but no misprint. Had you lived in his day, you may have wondered about his sanity! He was the kind of man who just wouldn't "get in line." His world was corrupt, but he believed in personal purity, of all things! How strange . . . yet how significant! We may not be familiar with him, but we surely understand his times.

He's a man who was surrounded by a moral fog. His book is an ancient call for repentance. It is a holy cry to God for divine intervention. And it's not just a cry; it's more like a scream. He says:

> How long, O LORD, will I call for help,
> And Thou wilt not hear?
> I cry out to Thee, "Violence!"
> Yet Thou dost not save (Habakkuk 1:2).

He saw immoral and brutal acts of violence. So, of course, he asked, "Why?" He also asked, "How long?" He struggled with God's lack of immediate action. Though the prophet prayed, God seemed unusually distant. "How long? Why?" The heavens were brass. "Why don't You act decisively? Why don't You unfold Your arms and get with it in this old, polluted world of ours? How long before You deliver Your people, Lord?" He continues:

> Why dost Thou make me see iniquity,
> And cause me to look on wickedness?
> Yes, destruction and violence are before me;
> Strife exists and contention arises.
> Therefore, the law is ignored
> And justice is never upheld.
> For the wicked surround the righteous;
> Therefore, justice comes out perverted (vv. 3–4).

> Art Thou not from everlasting,
> O LORD, my God, my Holy One?
> We will not die (v. 12a).

"I thought You were holy. Aren't You the Holy One? Then how in the world can You sit back and do so little about my unholy world?" "[Habakkuk] could not reconcile a bad world with a holy God."[3]

How bad was his world? As we just observed, it was a world of brutal violence (v. 2) so severe that the prophet screamed out his prayer. It was a world of personal iniquity and wickedness (v. 3).

"Why dost Thou make me see *iniquity?*" The word includes lying, vanity, and idolatry. "Why do You cause me to look on *wickedness?*" That Hebrew term encompasses oppression, robbery, and assault.

There were crimes of homicide going on in the streets. "Aren't You Jehovah of Judah? Aren't You the God of this nation? Where are You, God?"

There were strife and relational wrangling. There were arguments in homes, fights between parents and kids as well as between marital partners—not to mention disputes between bosses and employees. And did you notice another relevant issue? The law was not being upheld. Even when it was, it was being compromised. What a scene! It's going to sound familiar: brutal violence, personal iniquity, relational wrangling, legal compromise. You'd think Habakkuk lived in the inner city of some American metropolis.

I smiled when I was listening to a rather well-known Bible expositor a while back. He said he'd just completed a serious study into the fourth, fifth, and sixth centuries B.C. and found himself intrigued to discover what they wrestled with back then.

He mentioned five issues that concerned those ancient people: (1) the imminent outbreak of international hostility; (2) the breakup of homes—weakening marriages; (3) the rebellion of youth and their lack of respect for parents or for the elderly; (4) the corruption in politics—integrity was undermined; and (5) the chuck-holes in the public roads!

Does that sound familiar? Does it sound like something you could identify with? History certainly has a way of repeating itself.

That's what makes Habakkuk's complaint so timely. "I thought You were holy, God! Where are You? How can You allow this to happen? I'm surrounded by a fog of moral pollution, and I'm tired of breathing it in. I'm tired of its diseased impact on my life. I'm beginning to wonder about a holy God in a world of people *this* unholy." Maybe those are your sentiments, too.

Habakkuk cried aloud. Another prophet, named Jeremiah, just quietly sobbed. I have in mind his words as recorded in Jeremiah 6. He lived a little later than Habakkuk, though not much. Habakkuk feared the nation's demise; Jeremiah actually lived to see it happen.

That's why he wrote Lamentations, which is another name for *weeping*. Appropriately, Jeremiah is called "the weeping prophet." He doesn't scream. He doesn't fight. He doesn't even argue. He just sobs. He writes his prophecy while wiping tears from his eyes.

> *"Be warned, O Jerusalem,*
> *Lest I be alienated from you;*
> *Lest I make you a desolation,*
> *A land not inhabited" (Jeremiah 6:8).*

> *To whom shall I speak and give warning,*
> *That they may hear?*
> *Behold, their ears are closed (v. 10a).*

Understand, that's the result of living in the fog. "The system" takes its toll. Your ears slowly become closed, so much so that you can't hear the spiritual message God is giving. *"They cannot listen."* Observe the way Jeremiah puts it:

> *The word of the LORD has become a reproach to them;*
> *They have no delight in it (v. 10b).*

Do you want to know how that sounds in today's terms? "Aw, c'mon . . . get off that stuff! Get up with the times, man! All that prophet-of-doom talk is old hat. This is where it's at!" In Jeremiah's words, *"They have no delight in it"*—that is, in hearing the truth about holiness.

> *But I am full of the wrath of the LORD: I am weary* *with holding it in (v. 11a).*

"I'm boiling. I'm churning . . . I'm so tired, Lord."

> *For from the least of them even to the greatest of them,* *Everyone is greedy for gain (v. 13a).*

Does that sound familiar?

Again, these verses describe life as it is lived in a moral fog. There is a constant fighting for gain. There's competition to get more and more.

And to make matters worse:

> *From the prophet even to the priest*
> *Everyone deals falsely (v. 13b).*

Jeremiah weeps, "It's bad enough that it's in the law courts, but it's now in the pulpits, Lord. It's to the place where I can't trust the one who wears a collar, who says he speaks for You. I can't be sure that those who are robed with the mantle of God tell me the truth anymore. They deal falsely. They have healed the wound of Your people just slightly." Look at what he says! "They keep saying, 'Shalom, shalom!' when there is no shalom! There isn't any peace. But they keep saying, 'Don't worry. Don't worry. It's gonna be okay,' when it's *not* going to be okay."

And if you don't think *that's* bad, look at verse 15.

> *"Were they ashamed because of the abomination they*
> *   have done?*
> *They were not even ashamed at all;*
> *They did not even know how to blush."*

Honestly now, did you know the Bible spoke of a time in history when people were so caught up in an immoral lifestyle that they no longer blushed? Jeremiah sobs, "I notice, God, that there are no more red faces. No one seems shocked anymore."

Today I suppose we could call it compensating or maybe rationalizing. In order to handle the shock of our day, we compensate by remaining free of shock. I repeat, that's part of living in the fog.

Psychiatrist Karl Menninger took up the pen of a prophet when he wrote *Whatever Became of Sin?* In that searching book he admits, "In a discussion of the sin of *lust* we have to allow for a considerable shift in the social code during the past century. It has been called a revolution, and perhaps it is. Many forms of sexual activity which for centuries were considered reprehensible, immoral, and sinful *anywhere*, and their public exhibition simply *anathema*, are now talked and written about and exhibited on the stage and screen."[4]

From *Honesty, Morality, and Conscience* by Jerry White, I find a similar concern:

> We live in the age of freedom of expression and freedom of lifestyle. X-rated movies and magazines are available in every city. Legislation to control pornography has failed in most places. The sexual fiction of yesterday is the reality of today. Magazines displayed in supermarkets present articles featuring unmarried couples living together. Sex manuals advocate extramarital affairs. Fewer and fewer teenagers leave high school as virgins. Prime-time television flaunts homosexuality and infidelity.[5]

Pitirim Sorokin, formerly professor of sociology at Harvard, laments:

> There has been a growing preoccupation of our writers with the social sewers, the broken homes of disloyal parents and unloved children, the bedroom of the prostitute, a cannery row brothel, a den of criminals, a ward of the insane, a club of dishonest politicians, a street corner gang of teenage delinquents, a hate-laden prison, a crime-ridden waterfront, the courtroom of a dishonest judge, the sex adventures of urbanized cavemen and rapists, the loves of adulterers and fornicators, of masochists, sadists, prostitutes, mistresses, playboys. Juicy loves, ids, orgasms, and libidos are seductively prepared and served with all the trimmings.[6]

And to add Jeremiah's observation: Nobody blushes anymore. It's all part of the moral pollution . . . the fog. "The system" may be insidious, but it is effective.

In every major city today, with a turn of the television dial, you can bring explicit sex right into your home for anybody to watch. And nobody blushes.

You don't even have to go into an "adult" bookstore anymore to find pornography. You can find it in quick-stop grocery stores or in some large drugstores and supermarkets. You may have to look a little, but it's there. Again I remind you, nobody blushes.

The ultimate, telltale sign of a low view of personal holiness is that we no longer blush when we find wrong. Instead, we make jokes about it. We re-dress immorality and make it appear funny. And if we don't laugh, we're considered prudes . . . we're weird . . . we're kind of crotchety.

Maybe I don't like to laugh about that anymore because, as a minister, I am forced to deal with the consequences of it. And that's never funny. People in the backwash of a sensual lifestyle don't come to me and my staff to talk about the lasting joys of illicit sex. They wonder about their family; or what they should do about this disease; or how they can deal with this incestuous relationship that's tearing the home apart; or how they're going to tell their parents that she's pregnant out of wedlock, knowing it will break their parents' hearts.

It would be bad enough if it were limited to the world, but, as I mentioned in my introduction, it is now in the Church—the place most people would consider to be the ultimate bastion of holiness.

THE TRUTH: GOD'S TIMELESS COUNSEL FOR CHRISTIANS

I'm grateful that God talks straight when it comes to moral purity. I'm grateful He doesn't stutter or shuffle or shift His position. I'm even more grateful that He doesn't laugh. It's as if He is looking His people directly in the eye and lovingly, yet firmly, saying, "I want you to hear this very clearly. I'll make it brief and simple." Then He leaves us with a decision regarding personal holiness. Only one decision pleases Him—*obedience*.

As John Brown, a nineteenth-century Scottish theologian, once stated: "Holiness does not consist in mystic speculations, enthusiastic fervors, or uncommanded austerities; *it consists in thinking as God thinks and willing as God wills*."[7]

That's what the apostle Paul is asking of the reader in chapter 4 of 1 Thessalonians. He got his foot in the door in the last part of chapter 3 when he set forth a foundational guideline on how to *"really live"* as we *"stand firm in the Lord"* (v. 8). What does that include?

> *And may the Lord cause you to increase and abound in love for one another, and for all men, just as we also do for you; so that He may establish your hearts unblamable in holiness . . . (vv. 12–13a).*

What a great way to live—*"unblamable in holiness"*! Confident living is directly linked to being "unblamable." It's better than knowing the answers to all the questions on a test, or having plenty of money, or earning an advanced degree. There's no security like being free of blame. When we are established in holiness, living unblamable lives of moral purity, we can smile at life. We can take its pressures and enjoy its pleasures. Then, when marriage comes along, we can enjoy the partnership of the opposite sex, including all the joys of sexual delights.

Make no mistake about it, God is pleased when married partners enjoy a healthy sex life together. He applauds it. And why shouldn't He? He invented it. His Word clearly states that marriage is to be held in honor, and the marriage bed is to be undefiled—free of blame (Hebrews 13:4). But the implied warning is clear: If we remove sex from its original, God-given context, it becomes *"sexual immorality," "lustful passion,"* and *"impurity."*

IN YOUR WALK, EXCEL!
1 Thessalonians 4:1–2

> *Finally then, brethren, we request and exhort you in the Lord Jesus, that, as you received from us instruction as to how you ought to walk and please God (just as you actually do walk), that you may excel still more (v. 1).*

We have other ways of saying "excel" today: "Go for it. Give it your best shot. Don't just drift; pursue!" Or, as many parents often say, "Get with it!" Paul says, in effect, "Just as we have written you and have served as models before you, I encourage you to excel in your walk. *Get with it!* Make something happen in your life. Don't just drift along in a fog of mediocrity. Go the second mile. Excel!"

If you're a C student, try your best for a B. If you tend to be rather laid back in life, now's the time to go beyond your normal level. I exhort you to give yourself to diligence. Overcome that tendency toward laziness. All of that and more is involved in excelling.

While advocating an excelling lifestyle, Paul targets one specific area that needs constant attention: moral purity.

IN YOUR MORALS, ABSTAIN!
1 Thessalonians 4:3–6

For this is the will of God, your sanctification; that is, that you abstain from sexual immorality (v. 3).

Paul has written strong and emotional words regarding our spiritual walk. We are to excel in it. Now he specifies our moral life. Whoever wishes to excel in his or her spiritual walk must come to terms with an inner battle: sexual lust. (I'll say more about the specifics of fighting lust in the next chapter.) Yes, it IS a battle . . . a vicious, powerful, relentless fight that won't suddenly stop when we turn fifty. And it won't end just because we may lose our mate. Nor will it decrease because our geography changes, or because we are well educated, or because we may be isolated behind prison walls, or because we remain single, or even because we enter the ministry. The struggle to be morally pure is one of those issues from which no one is immune. That includes you! Now let's understand what God is saying here.

"This is the will of God." Very seldom will you find such straight talk in Scripture. When it comes to remaining morally pure, you don't need to pray and ask whether it's God's will. *"This is the will of God . . . abstain from sexual immorality."* That last word is translated from the Greek word *porneia*. Obviously, we get our words *pornography* or *pornographic* from that original term. It refers to any kind of intimate, sexual encounter apart from one's marital partner. It would include, of course, intimate encounters with the opposite sex or with the same sex. Fornication, adultery, or homosexuality would

be included in *porneia*. Clearly, the command is that we are to *abstain*. Abstain means exactly that—*abstain*. Outside marriage, have nothing to do with sexual involvements with others.

Now in the fog of horizontal standards, you will be left with any number of options. You will be told by some to be discreet, but certainly not to abstain. "I mean, let's not be fanatical about this." A few may even counsel you, "It would be dangerous for you to play around with somebody else's mate, so don't do that. And, for sure, you need to watch out for disease."

But wait. Abstain, in Scripture, doesn't simply mean "watch out" or "be discreet" or to indulge in "safe sex." It means *"have nothing to do"* with something. Others' advice continues: "It's unwise for you to cohabit with a partner in your family. That's incest." (It is not only unhealthy, but it is illegal.) "If you're a teacher, you shouldn't be intimate with your students. That's not professionally wise, so don't do that," some would caution. But again I remind you: Scripture clearly states that it is God's will that we abstain. Moral purity is a matter of abstaining, not simply being careful.

How relieving it is to know exactly where we stand with our holy God! Now then, let's be very specific: If you are not married, there are no sexual exceptions provided for you. It is the will of God that you not be sexually intimate with any other person until marriage. That's what Scripture teaches both here and elsewhere. That is how to walk in obedience. It is God's best. Furthermore, it is for your good, and it enhances God's glory.

I'm pleased to add that we are not left with simply a stark command. Amplifying counsel follows in verses 4 and 5:

> *That each of you know how to possess his own vessel in sanctification and honor, not in lustful passion, like the Gentiles who do not know God.*

It is God's will that we abstain from moral impurity. It is also His will that we know how to do that. I suggest that you must become a student of *yourself* in order to know how to handle your battle with sexual lust. Those who fail to know themselves will lose the battle and ultimately become enslaved to lust. In order for one to *"possess his own vessel,"* there must be a practical, working knowledge of one's own tendencies.

You know what kind of student you are, academically, in order to pass the course. You have to apply what you know will work in order to pass the test, and accomplish the course, and get the degree or the diploma, correct? In the realm of your intimate life, there must be another equally diligent application of knowledge. Each of us is to know how to *"possess his own vessel"*—meaning, maintain purity in one's own body.

The point? In order to abstain from *porneia*, we must become alert and disciplined students of our bodies: how they function, what appeals to them, and what weakens as well as strengthens them. We are to know how to control our inner drive, how to gain mastery over it, and how to sustain ourselves in a life of purity rather than yielding to lustful passions.

Let me amplify that by putting it in practical words no one can possibly misunderstand. Within the media, there are certain things that you and I cannot handle. We are to know ourselves well enough to admit that and to face the fact that certain sensual stimuli weaken us. We simply cannot tolerate those things and stay pure. The obvious conclusion is this: We are wrong to traffic in them. There are certain magazines you and I should not read. There are certain films, television programs, and late-night channels we have no business watching. There are certain people who, by their suggestive conversation, weaken us. There are settings too tempting, touches too personal, and liberties that are too much for us to handle. We are fools to play around with them. They create appealing temptations we simply cannot control. So, if we are committed to abstain, we stay clear of them.

Such decisions are difficult to make and even more difficult to implement, but it is all part of our knowing how to *"possess [our vessels] in sanctification and honor."* Remember this: No one automatically remains morally pure. Abstention from sexual immorality is never an easy-come, easy-go issue. As I said earlier, it's like combat. We're talking *warfare!*

The battle rages in the realm of sexually stimulating activities. Even some parties, places, kinds of music, and pastimes can weaken us. Again, we are fools to tolerate those things. A person who is trying to recover from alcoholism realizes he is fighting a losing battle if he chooses to live on the second floor above a bar. No question about it, it will lead to failure. There is more:

> *And that no man transgress and defraud his brother in*
> *the matter because the Lord is the avenger in all these things,*
> *just as we also told you before and solemnly warned you (v. 6).*

Some would get around total sexual abstention by saying, "Well, what we could do is just keep this within the family. It's okay if it's between two family members or among Christians." But He corners us here as well. He adds that *"no [one] transgress and defraud his brother in the matter, because the Lord is the avenger in all these things."*

This verse refers not only to members in the family of God but to individual family members—the indecent practices of relating intimately to one's daughter or daughter-in-law, son or son-in-law, mother, stepmother, father, stepfather, and on and on, covering the whole realm of incest. Such indecent, unlawful acts defraud our family members!

Now to state it painfully straight: God clearly and unequivocally stands against extramarital sex, homosexual sex, and sexual encounters with individuals outside of marriage under ANY situation. I repeat, the command is direct and dogmatic:

> *"Abstain from sexual immorality."*

As I write this, I realize I am not the only one saying these things. But, I confess, sometimes I feel like a lonely voice in our day. And because some illustrations could appear as gossip, I choose not to use anyone else but myself as an example. Allow me to tell you *my* story.

My wife and I were married in June of 1955. We both were quite young. I finished my schooling and then faced the need to fulfill my military obligation. Back in the 1950s, the military was not an option to choose but a requirement to be fulfilled. Because their time requirement best suited my particular situation, I chose the Marine Corps . . . an outfit not known for its moral purity.

I received the promise from my recruiting officer that if I joined, I would not have to serve my military duty overseas. Since I was married, that certainly was appealing to me because I was enjoying life with my bride, and the last thing we wanted was a forced separation from each other. I really wanted to be with her. But, through a chain of events too lengthy to explain, I would up eight thousand miles from home. Stationed in the Orient for over a year, I was suddenly faced with sexual temptation as I had never known it.

Before I ever dropped the sea bag off my shoulder on the island of Okinawa, I was faced with a tough decision. I was going to make my home in barracks characterized by a godless lifestyle. Venereal disease was not uncommon among those on the island. Living with a woman in the village was as common as breathing smog in southern California. If you lived in Okinawa, you slept around. And it wasn't uncommon for the chaplain, who was supposed to lecture incoming marines about purity, to ultimately joke his way through and tell you where to go to get penicillin shots. Welcome to the real world, Swindoll.

I realized, especially since I had known the joys of intimacy in marriage, that temptation would be incredibly strong. Surrounded by men who couldn't have cared less about the things of God, away from my home and free from physical accountability to my wife and my family, I would soon become another nameless marine in the back alleys of Okinawan villages. But I was a Christian. I determined then and there to *"abstain from sexual immorality."* How I praise my Lord for His sustaining strength!

By the grace of God, the decision that I made back in the late 1950s allows me to speak and write today with confidence. Had I not been preserved from unfaithfulness, I would have to pass rather hurriedly and embarrassingly over this passage and similar sections of Scripture. I sincerely doubt that I would have pursued the ministry had I fallen into sexual lust.

Candidly, I had to be tough on myself. There were times when I had to be downright *brutal* with my emotions. I had to make some tough, Spartan decisions . . . unpopular decisions among a bunch of guys who tried everything in the book to tempt me. I was determined to be different so that I could reach those fellow marines with a message that had integrity.

Let me clarify something, lest you misunderstand. God showed me it wasn't my job to clean up the goldfish bowl; it was my job to fish. I wasn't called to lead a flag-waving crusade for moral purity across the Orient. It was my job to live clean whether anybody else did or not. To put it bluntly, I was not to put my hands on someone who wasn't my wife. I wasn't even to *talk* about such things. Today I can speak from experience when I write these words: Sexual abstention works. It pays rich and rewarding dividends. It works . . . even in the life of a young, red-blooded marine surrounded by endless opportunities to yield.

God made it clear to me that if I would abstain from sexual immorality, He would honor that. His Spirit came to my rescue time and again. I had no corner on strength. I was often in the path of temptation, as anyone reading these words right now would understand, but I refused to surrender. Those were lonely days away from home for almost eighteen months. I was often burning with desire for my wife. But, thank God, I was committed to abstaining from immorality.

How did I make it? I involved myself in things that were wholesome, things that paid off, things that kept me busy, active, and fulfilled. I cultivated my musical abilities by becoming much more proficient in several instruments. I was also involved in an aggressive athletic program, spending most of my spare time with men who were committed to the same wholesome objectives. In my mind, the village was "off limits." I didn't even drop in and get a soft drink in the village bars. I couldn't handle it. When I got off the bus that took me to my destination, I looked straight ahead and walked fast. That little island had physically attractive women and over five thousand places of prostitution. I never touched one of them. Obviously, I saw them . . . but I refused to yield.

In my heart I knew that once I broke, once I stepped into that sensual world, I would not stop. I knew the drive that was inside me *couldn't* be stopped once I yielded. I probably would not even have wanted to stop it. It's like breaking with a diet. Once you take off the restraint, it's much easier to say, "Who cares?" Once you've eaten a little chocolate cake following lunch, that night it's *half a pie!*

Perhaps you are thinking, "That just mocks me, because my lifestyle isn't there. I've already compromised sexually . . . I'm not walking in purity." Wait! My message to you isn't complicated—*start today!* It's time to take charge, my Christian friend. Telling yourself it won't work is the very thing that keeps you from a life of moral purity and its rewards. Stop lying to yourself! If you are born from above, if you are a child of God, then this passage is addressed to *you.* Your name belongs at the beginning of these verses.

See verse 1 of 1 Thessalonians 4. "Finally then, *brethren . . .*" Put your name there. This is specific instruction for you, child of God. No one else has the power. To be very frank with you, it's beyond me how an unsaved person can stay morally pure. Only by the power of the living Christ and His Spirit can this kind of life be carried out. If you really want to live in moral purity, yet you are not a Christian, then put first things first. You need to come to Christ. Becoming a Christian precedes cleaning up your moral act. Trusting in the Lord Jesus Christ is primary. Only then can you call upon the power you will need to walk in personal holiness.

Even then, I remind you, it won't be easy or automatic. You'll still need to apply the techniques I've mentioned to sustain your commitment to purity. I have found there are times when temptation is so fierce I have to be almost rude to the opposite sex. That may not sound very nice, but that's the price I'm willing to pay. It is worth it, believe me.

Some of you are husbands and fathers. The habits of fidelity you are forming directly affect your wife and children at home. How careful are you with personal holiness? How consistent? How tough are you on yourself? You cannot depend on anyone else to provide you with a moral standard. YOUR moral standard is the one that's going to keep you pure . . . or lead you astray. Isn't it time you become serious about moral purity?

You may be single, attractive, and capable. You may have entered a fine career. That's great . . . but it is also possible that you have begun to compromise your morals. You may find yourself saying, "It feels so good, and I am so lonely, and it is so accessible, so secret." Wait . . . it *isn't* secret! There is no "secret sin" before God. Furthermore, it won't remain a secret on earth forever.

See what it says in verse 6? It's not often that the Lord calls Himself the *Avenger,* but He does in this case. The meaning? "One who satisfies justice by punishing or disciplining the wrongdoer." Not all of that avenging will wait until the judgment day. Some of it happens now in the form of anxiety, conflict, guilt, disease, insanity . . . even death.

By the way, 1 Corinthians 6:18 is a pretty significant verse. In a context much like the one we've been considering, the writer exhorts the reader not to compromise morally. The verse says:

> *Flee immorality. Every other sin that a man commits is outside the body, but the immoral man sins against his own body.*

Practically speaking, all other sins can be fairly well managed in an objective manner. But this one comes in on you. In today's terms, it's an "inside job." In many ways, sexual sins take a personal toll on the victim, leaving the person in bondage, increasingly less satisfied, and on a downward spiral which only results in greater tragedy.

Few have ever said it better than evangelist Billy Graham:

> In every area of our social life we see operating the inevitable law of diminishing returns in our obsession with sex. Many do something for a thrill only to find the next time that they must increase the dose to produce the same thrill. As the kick wears off, they are driven to look for new means, for different experiences to produce a comparable kick. The sex glutton is tormented by feelings of guilt and remorse. His mode of living is saturated with intense strain, unnatural emotions, and inner conflicts. His personality is thwarted in its search for development. His passions are out of control, and the end result is frustration. In his defiance of God's law and society's norm, he puts a death-dealing tension on his soul.

His search for new thrills, for new kicks, for exciting experiences keeps him in the grip of fear, insecurity, doubt, and futility. Dr. Sorokin says: "The weakened physical, emotional, and spiritual condition of the sex glutton usually makes him incapable of resisting the accompanying pressures, and he eventually cracks under their weight. He often ends by becoming a psychoneurotic or suicide."[8]

When just a small boy, I remember memorizing the following:

> Sow a thought, and you reap an act;
> Sow an act, and you reap a habit;
> Sow a habit, and you reap a character;
> Sow a character, and you reap a destiny.

How true! And we never come to the place where we can call a halt to the sowing-reaping process.

I heard of a Christian leader who interviewed a veteran missionary who was then in his eighties. The interviewer asked, "Tell me, when did you get beyond the problem with lust?" In candor the godly gentleman answered, "It hasn't happened yet. The battle still goes on!" If you're waiting to outgrow the battle, don't hold your breath.

IN YOUR REASONING, REMEMBER!
1 Thessalonians 4:7–8

For God has not called us for the purpose of impurity, but in sanctification (v. 7).

Paul uses "sanctification" for the third time in this passage. It's a theological term referring to our pilgrimage, our progress from earth to heaven. Perhaps we could call it our growth pattern.

Remember this: You and I have been called to operate in the sphere of spiritual progress. God has called us to be in a spiritual growth pattern. Sometimes we're up . . . sometimes down. Sometimes we're more victorious than other times. But the progress is a movement forward and higher. God certainly has *not* called us for the purpose of impurity, even though we continue to live in a world socked in by a moral fog.

Consequently, he who rejects this is not rejecting man but the God who gives His Holy Spirit to you (v. 8).

The second thing to remember is: To reject a lifestyle of holiness is to reject the God who empowers you to live it. Holy living is inseparably linked to believing in a holy God.

THE CHOICE: A DECISION ONLY YOU CAN MAKE

Let me conclude my thoughts by simplifying your options. Actually, you have two. First, you can choose to live your life in a horizontal fog. If that is your choice, the results are predictable. You will continue to drift in a thick mist of moral uncertainties. Your disobedience will result in a series of rationalizations that will leave you empty. Guilt and grief will be your companions. You can choose to live like that. If you do, you open up a door of misery for yourself. You'll play at church. You'll toss around a few religious words. But before very long, your lifestyle will match the atmosphere around you. Your eyes will no longer tear up. Your conscience will no longer sting. Your heart won't beat faster. You may even stop blushing. A jaded, horizontal lifestyle is an option. But it has those consequences . . . those terrible consequences.

Why? The Avenger. God doesn't let His children play in the traffic without getting hurt. Your disobedience will result in increasing personal misery.

Second, you can choose to live your life vertically on target. The benefits? You will honor the God of moral absolutes. And your obedience will result in greater personal confidence and habits of holiness. It will begin to come supernaturally. You'll find yourself stronger, more secure, possessing a healthy self-image.

Internally, we're a little like an automobile. The God who made us built us with all the right lights on our internal dashboard. I don't know of anybody who, after purchasing a new car, also buys a little hammer for the glove compartment. Let's imagine a weird scene. Let's say that as two men are driving along, one of the lights on the dashboard starts flashing red. The driver says to his friend,

"Hand me that hammer in the glove compartment, okay? Thanks."
Tap . . . Tap . . . Bamm . . . Bamm . . . Pow! "There! Now we've
gotten rid of *that* light." Smoke is coming out of the hood, yet the
guy keeps driving along.

How foolish! And yet, it isn't difficult to find people who will
hand out hammers. As they do, they say, "Aw, that's needless guilt.
We're in an age where guilt is no longer considered important. You
need to get rid of all that stuff." But wait . . . that's NECESSARY
guilt! God help us when we don't have it! It's the conscience that
bites into us deep within and stings us when we compromise our
moral purity. When we sin, it's supposed to hurt. We are supposed
to be miserable when we compromise morally. That's the red light
flashing down inside. It's God's way of saying, "Pull over . . . stop.
Lift the hood. Deal with the real problem."

Jonathan Edwards, one of the great preachers of early
American history, once made this resolution: "*Resolved*, Never to do
any thing, which I should be afraid to do if it were the last hour of
my life."[9]

You have available to you the power that's necessary to solve
the real problems of your life. He is Jesus Christ. And once you
have the Savior, you also have the Holy Spirit. He will come inside
not to mock you but to help you; not simply to cry with you over
how strong the temptation is but to empower you to overcome it.
You can do all things through Him who keeps on pouring His
power into you. Even if you have never done it in your life, you
can begin a life of power today. There's no checklist. There's no
probation period. There's no long list of responsibilities that you
must fulfill before God will give you the power.

Been in the fog too long? Come on out. Enjoy the sunshine.

*Holy Father in Heaven, our world is a difficult one in which to
live. The fog is thick, and the heat is stifling. It's difficult . . . but not
impossible. Thankfully, Your power provides us with hope . . . hope to
start anew, even though we have failed; hope to press on, even though
we are afraid; hope to walk in moral purity, even though we are weak.*

I pray for all who have read this chapter. I pray that You would use it to turn their hearts toward You . . . to help them break the syndrome of immorality, to find true freedom, happiness, and holiness by hearing Your Word, obeying Your counsel, and walking in Your truth. In the invincible name of Jesus Christ,

Amen.

CHAPTER SIX

RESISTING THE LURE OF LUST

As we noted in the last chapter, red-blooded, healthy American men and women struggle with the same savage—lust. Non-Christians and Christians alike grapple with its presence and its persistence throughout their lives. Some think that getting married will cause temptation to flee. It doesn't. Others have tried isolation. But sensual imagination goes with them, fighting and clawing for attention and gratification. Not even being called into vocational Christian service helps. Ask any whose career is in the Lord's work. Temptation is there, relentlessly pleading for satisfaction.

In the previous chapter we took a wide-angle look at the problem of moral purity, then began to zoom in on that daily battle each one of us must fight in the private corners of our personal lives. Let's continue that look—that close-hand look at one of life's greatest potential stress fractures.

"How do I cope with moral temptation? How do I say no when lust screams yes? Can I conquer this sensual savage?" These are questions most people ask . . . but they go unanswered. We reach out for help, but seldom find it. To make matters worse, we are surrounded by folks who believe the only way to handle temptation is to yield to it. Stupid advice!

The Bible doesn't dodge the tough issues. It offers plain, achievable counsel that works. It promises hope, power, and assurance for those

who are weary of losing the battle and living with guilt.
   So does this chapter.

———◆———

Olympic hockey hero Jim Craig thought he had his hands
full during the Americans' gold-medal-winning perfor-
mance against a mighty Soviet opponent. The pressure of
the 1980 Winter Olympics was immense for the goalie and his
plucky teammates . . . but the real ordeal began afterwards.

   People's demands from all over the country increased with
crushing impact. His name became a household word in the homes
of sports fans around the world. Offers and opportunities were an
almost-everyday occurrence. The temptations were also frequent.
A local newspaper reported:

> . . . Craig now admits that the pace was so frantic that he
> developed an ulcer. . . .
>   Jim Naughton of the New York Times wrote:
> "There was the time in Chicago when he unlocked his
> hotel room to find a nude woman lying on his bed (Craig
> said, 'Please leave.') . . .
>   "There was an occasion in Chicago when he awoke
> with the feeling that someone was watching him, and
> glancing to the door, he saw four female hotel employees
> peering around the door. ('I always use the bolt now.')
> There was the time in Atlanta when a girl who said she
> had been speaking to God about him kissed him pas-
> sionately . . . and then passed out."[1]

   No one is immune to temptation. Not even a hero. Not even
a nobody. Not even people like you and me. Lust is never very far
away. And just when you least expect it, there it is again.

TEMPTATION IN THREE DIMENSIONS

   Temptations come packaged in varied shapes, sizes, and colors, but most of them fall into one of three categories:
   1. *Material Temptation.* This is lust for things. The things may

be as large as a house or as small as a ring, as bright and dazzling as a new sports car, or as dull and dusty as a two-hundred-year-old antique dresser.

2. *Personal Temptation.* This is lust for status. Special recognition. The status of fame, fortune, power, or authority. Having a title that makes heads turn, like "top executive" or "president" or "executive director" or even "doctor."

3. *Sensual Temptation.* This is lust for another person. The desire to have and enjoy the body of an individual, even though such pleasure is illegal and/or immoral. In this chapter, we'll limit our thoughts to this third category. Even though we shall do that, don't think for a minute that this one area is all there is to temptation. Sensuality is a large part of the battle, but it is by no means the whole story of the conflict within.

HISTORICAL SITUATION: A MAN NAMED JOSEPH

Rather than skate on the ice of theory and try to analyze temptation from an abstract viewpoint, let's plunge into the life of one who faced it head-on. His name is Joseph. His story is told in the book of Genesis, chapters 37 through 50. Of special interest to us is chapter 39, when lust paid the man an unexpected and unforgettable visit.

Joseph became the trusted slave of a high-ranking Egyptian official named Potiphar. Joseph was Jewish, a handsome young man who earlier had been hated and rejected by his brothers. They, by the way, had sold him into slavery, if you can believe it. Although a man of high principle and true godliness, Joseph became a common slave in Egypt.

Listen to the story as it unfolds:

> *Now Joseph had been taken down to Egypt; and Potiphar, an Egyptian officer of Pharaoh, the captain of the bodyguard, bought him from the Ishmaelites, who had taken him down there. And the LORD was with Joseph, so he became a successful man. And he was in the house of his master, the Egyptian. Now his master saw that the LORD was with him and how the LORD caused all that he did to prosper in his hand.*

So Joseph found favor in his sight, and became his personal servant; and he made him overseer over his house, and all that he owned he put in his charge. And it came about that from the time he made him overseer in his house, and over all that he owned, the LORD blessed the Egyptian's house on account of Joseph; thus the LORD's blessing was upon all that he owned, in the house and in the field. So he left everything he owned in Joseph's charge; and with him there he did not concern himself with anything except the food which he ate. Now Joseph was handsome in form and appearance (Genesis 39:1–6).

Potiphar had a very responsible position. As "captain of the bodyguard," he was in charge of that elite group of men who surrounded the Pharaoh and other Egyptian officials with protection. Perhaps it could be compared to our director of the Federal Bureau of Investigation. He was a respected, busy, well-paid officer. With a discerning eye, he had bought Joseph off the slave market, having seen in this fine young man the marks of maturity and responsibility. As time passed, Joseph was promoted to the very important position of "overseer." By and by, he was put in charge of all that Potiphar owned.

Two things stand out in these six verses that give us such a clear, historical backdrop:

1. The Lord was with Joseph.

Joseph didn't talk about it, but the truth couldn't be ignored. His master saw it. Whatever Joseph was given to do got done, and got done well.

2. Because of Joseph, the Lord prospered Potiphar.

Scripture states ". . . the LORD blessed the Egyptian's house on account of Joseph; thus the LORD's blessing was upon all that he owned . . ." (v. 5).

Promotions were well deserved. Finally, the top spot was granted to Joseph: house steward—Potiphar's personal and trusted confidant. He was the reason Potiphar had no worries.

Let it also be remembered that this series of promotions made Joseph increasingly more vulnerable. With greater success comes greater privileges and privacy. Wise is the old saint who wrote:

> We may expect temptation in days of prosperity and ease rather than in those of privation and toil. Not on the glacier slopes of the Alps, but in the sunny plains . . . not where men frown, but where they smile sweet exquisite smiles of flattery—it is there, it is there, that the temptress lies in wait! Beware! If thou goest armed anywhere, thou must, above all, go armed here.[2]

Joseph was a "sitting duck" for the appealing and flattering lure of lust. Perhaps it is because of this that the passage we've been looking at ends with the words, "Now Joseph was handsome in form and appearance" (Genesis 39:6). The Living Bible renders it: "Joseph, by the way, was a very handsome young man." The New International Version says, "Now Joseph was well-built and handsome."

Please understand that there is nothing wrong with a man being handsome and well built. (It isn't fair, but there's nothing evil about it.) It's like being wealthy—not necessarily wrong, it just intensifies the battle, for there will always be others who notice and drop the bait of lust . . . which is precisely what happened to Joseph.

SENSUAL TEMPTATION: ENTER MRS. POTIPHAR

And it came about after these events that his master's wife looked with desire at Joseph, and she said, "Lie with me" (Genesis 39:7).

Now that's what you could call the direct approach. The Hebrew says the woman "lifted up her eyes," which conveys the thought of paying close or special attention to him. She had been watching Joseph, imagining how enjoyable it would be to have him hold her and make love to her. With time on her hands, Mrs. Potiphar allowed lust to dominate her mind. She put the moves on this handsome, muscular young man and fully expected him to melt into her arms with passion.

Egyptologists and archaeologists alike verify that ancient Egyptian women were among the first to consider themselves "liberated." Egyptian monuments offer mute testimony to the extreme laxity of the morals of Egyptian women. This may explain her bold and shameless proposition.

Joseph's response must have shocked the woman. Look at verses 8 and 9.

But he refused and said to his master's wife, "Behold, with me here, my master does not concern himself with anything in the house, and he has put all that he owns in my charge. There is no one greater in this house than I, and he has withheld nothing from me except you, because you are his wife. How then could I do this great evil, and sin against God?"

As abrupt as her invitation had been, Joseph rejected. No way would he yield! But how could he resist? She was available. They could easily have guaranteed their secrecy. He was unmarried—and certainly a man with a strong sexual drive. How could he reject her offer?

Look closely at those verses you just read.

- He rejected her offer on the basis of *reason*. How foolish to break the trust he had been building for years! (v. 8).
- He rejected on the basis of *conscience* as well. It was unthinkable that he could violate the name of his God by yielding to her advances (v. 9).

Do you think she gave up? Not on your life. The next verse states she poured it on—"day after day." It also tells us he kept on refusing her persistent appeals. It even says he stopped listening to her and stopped being with her. He stayed away.

We admire the man. He was so determined not to yield that he took practical steps to keep lust at arm's length. Smart move!

Anyone who has played with lust can testify that it plays for keeps. Like fire, it will finally burn you. Here's why:

In our members there is a slumbering inclination towards desire which is both sudden and fierce. With irresistible power desire seizes mastery over the flesh. All at once a secret, smoldering fire is kindled. The flesh burns and is in flames. It makes no difference whether it is sexual desire, or ambition, or vanity, or desire for revenge, or love of fame and power, or greed for money, or finally, that strange desire for the beauty of the world of nature. Joy in God is . . . extinguished in us and we seek all our joy in the creature. At this moment God is quite unreal to us, he loses all reality, and only desire for the creature is real; the only reality is the devil. Satan does not here fill us with hatred of God, but with forgetfulness of God. . . . The lust thus aroused envelops the mind and will of man in deepest darkness. The powers of clear discrimination and of decision are taken from us. . . . It is here that everything within me rises up against the Word of God.[3]

Joseph was smart enough to realize that his "slumbering inclination" would indeed become a sudden and fierce savage, demanding gratification, if he listened to her offers. Would he simply "forget God" for awhile and enjoy? No, he stood his ground.

She still didn't quit. Read on.

> *Now it happened one day that he went into the house to do his work, and none of the men of the household was there inside. And she caught him by his garment, saying, "Lie with me!" And he left his garment in her hand and fled, and went outside (Genesis 39:11–12).*

The Hebrew says he left her and fled "to the street." He was out of there! He'd tried to reason with her, and she ignored his rationale. He'd tried to avoid her and spurn her advances, and she refused to honor his determination to remain pure. Now the only thing left to do was to bolt for the exit. Literally, he ran.

You may be surprised to know that every time the subject of sensual lust is discussed in the New Testament, there is one invariable command—RUN! We are told to get out, to flee, to run for our lives. It is impossible to yield to temptation while running in the opposite direction.

THE PRICE TAGS FOR PURITY

We've all heard the saying, "Heaven hath no rage like love to hatred turned, nor hell a fury like a woman scorned." And Mrs. Potiphar is certainly no exception! Not only scorned, she had been humiliated. Enraged and furious, she manufactured a lie with circumstantial evidence in her favor.

> *When she saw that he had left his garment in her hand, and had fled outside, she called to the men of her household, and said to them, "See, he has brought in a Hebrew to us to make sport of us; he came in to me to lie with me, and I screamed. And it came about when he heard that I raised my voice and screamed, that he left his garment beside me and fled, and went outside" (Genesis 39:13–15).*

Claiming to have been raped, she says that Joseph forced himself upon her and then ran. Her husband believes her (perhaps not completely, since he did not have Joseph killed) and locked him up in prison. Joseph did not remain there, however . . . but that's another part of this incredible story we haven't the time or space to tell.

What are the personal ramifications of all this for us living in today's world? How does it apply? Rather than pass it off with a vague "Lord, help us all" prayer, let me declare four "musts" based on Joseph's experience. These "musts" are to be applied if you expect to resist sensual temptations in your life.

1. *You must not be weakened by your situation.*

Economically, Joseph was secure, respected, trusted, and stable. Personally, he was handsome and desirable. He was also in charge of the entire house, so getting alone posed no problem. On top of all that, it wasn't his idea; the woman thought it up! And he was also unmarried.

Your flesh, creative and cool as it is, will invariably remind you of a dozen ways to rationalize around the wrong of your lust. There is a name for those who listen to those reasons: *victim*. You will yield if you allow yourself to be weakened.

2. *You must not be deceived in the persuasion.*

Remember Bonhoeffer's words? When lust reaches fever pitch, "God is quite unreal to us" and Satan fills us with "forgetfulness of God." This is a classic example of our adversary's deceptive methods. He attempts to cancel out tomorrow's consequences by emphasizing today's delights.

Joseph could have allowed himself to listen to the wrong voice. Men filled with lust do so every day:

"Her husband doesn't meet her needs like I can."

"Who will ever find out? We're safe."

"Look, we're going to be married soon."

"I'm so lonely. God will understand and forgive."

"Just this once—never, ever again."

Don't be deceived by such persuasive thoughts. Once again, rivet the clear command of God we highlighted in the last chapter:

> *For this is the will of God, your sanctification: that is, that you abstain from sexual immorality (1 Thessalonians 4:3).*

3. *You must not be gentle with your emotions.*

Look again at Joseph's model (Genesis 39):

Verse 8: *He refused.*

Verse 9: *How then could I do this great evil . . .?*

Verse 10: *He did not listen to her to lie beside her, or be with her.*

Verse 12: *He left . . . and fled. . . .*

Be tough on yourself; boldly reject the bait! Think of it as a brutal savage, ready to pounce and devour.

> . . . Lust is committed to wage war against your soul—in a life-and-death struggle—in hand-to-hand combat. Don't stand before this mortal enemy and argue or fight in your own strength—run for cover. . . . Lust is one flame you dare not fan. You'll get burned if you do.[4]

When it comes to your emotions, be tough rather than tender. Refuse to let your feelings dominate your mind when lust craves satisfaction.

4. *You must not be confused with the immediate results.*

Do you recall what happened to our friend Joseph? Even though he resisted the woman's advances, she kept coming back. Instead of those advances tapering off, they intensified. Instead of being immediately rewarded for his self-control, he was falsely accused and dumped into a dungeon. Talk about confusing!

But Joseph kept his eyes fixed on the Lord. He refused to be disillusioned. How often I've seen people withstand a barrage of temptation for awhile, then in a weak moment fall because of confusion! The enemy does not surrender easily. Keep standing firm, even though you feel strangely alone and forgotten by the Lord. Ultimately, He will reward every act of moral restraint.

SCRIPTURAL ANALYSIS OF TEMPTATION

Three New Testament passages come to mind when I think of any temptation, including sensuality: Matthew 4:1–11, 1 Corinthians 10:13, and James 1:13–16. Each one emphasizes an important truth that helps us counteract our tendency to yield when tempted. By analyzing each, we'll get a better handle on the problem.

Matthew 4:1–11

This is the familiar account of the time when the devil tempted Christ. He launched his full-scale attack on the Son of God. But Jesus never yielded. Why? What was it that gave Him such inner strength? Read these eleven verses in your Bible, slowly and aloud. You will hear yourself saying the same words three times:

> . . . it is written . . . (v. 4),
> . . . it is written . . . (v. 7),
> . . . it is written . . . (v. 10).

Following those words, each time Jesus referred back to verses of Scripture from the Old Testament—Deuteronomy 8:3, Deuteronomy 6:16, and Deuteronomy 6:13. When the Lord Jesus Christ was tempted, He used the Word of God, which He quoted aloud from memory.

Interestingly, only one offensive weapon is part of our armor described in Ephesians 6:10–17, "the sword of the Spirit, which is the word of God." The Greek term translated "word" is the term meaning "saying." It has reference to something *spoken*.

Let's take that literally! Christ did. He actually *stated* the words from Scripture. He "wielded" the sword of the Spirit in the face of the tempter. God honored His truth. We read in Matthew 4:11—immediately following the third time Jesus had quoted Scripture—*then the devil left Him. . . .*

If you want to stand strong against the magnetic, powerful lure of lust, quote aloud the Word of God. The psalmist is correct:

> *How can a young man keep his way pure? By keeping it according to Thy word.*
> *With all my heart I have sought Thee; Do not let me wander from Thy commandments.*
> *Thy word I have treasured in my heart, That I may not sin against Thee (Psalm 119:9–11).*

A pure heart is directly linked to "treasuring God's Word" there.

First Corinthians 10:13

The apostle Paul gives us hope in this verse of Scripture.

> *No temptation has overtaken you but such as is common to man; and God is faithful, who will not allow you to be tempted beyond what you are able, but with the temptation will provide the way of escape also, that you may be able to endure it.*

A close look at these words reveals something we tend to forget when we're tempted: God is there through it all. He is faithful. We may feel alone, but we are not alone. He places definite limitations on the attack, not allowing the magnet to be stronger than we can bear. And He also promised to provide "the way of escape" so that we aren't totally surrounded and consumed by the temptation. Left completely to ourselves, abandoned and forgotten by God, we would have no hope of victory. But God is faithful. He doesn't leave us in the lurch. Never!

I once heard a father tells of his son's first serious conflict at school. His boy was being picked on by two or three bullies. They punched the youngster a time or two, pushed him over when he was riding his bike home from school, and generally made life miserable for the lad. They told him they would meet him the next morning and beat him up.

That evening the dad really worked with the boy at home. He showed him how to defend himself, passed along a few helpful techniques, and even gave him some tips on how he might try to win them over as friends. The next morning the lad and dad prayed together, knowing the inevitable was sure to happen. With a reassuring embrace and a firm handshake, the father smiled confidently and said, "You can do it, son. I know you'll make out all right."

Choking back the tears, the boy got on his bike and began the long, lonely ride to school. What the boy did not know was that every block he rode, he was under the watchful eye of his dad . . . who drove his car a safe distance from his son, out of sight but ever ready to speed up and assist if the scene became too threatening. The boy thought he was alone, but he wasn't at all. The father was there all the time.

This, however, does not mean that God is actually involved in setting us up. In no way is He responsible for those temptations that fling themselves across our path. This brings me to the third significant biblical passage.

James 1:13–16

James, practical Christian that he is, spells out the downward spiral that occurs when we yield to temptation.

> Let no one say when he is tempted, "I am being tempted by God"; for God cannot be tempted by evil, and He Himself does not tempt anyone. But each one is tempted when he is carried away and enticed by his own lust. Then when lust has conceived, it gives birth to sin; and when sin is accomplished, it brings forth death. Do not be deceived, my beloved brethren.

As we think over these descriptive words, three facts emerge:

1. *Temptation is inevitable.* Did you notice the word *when* (v. 13)? We will never find a place that will secure us from all temptations. Not even the monk in the remotest monastery is safe. He may think he's protected, but his mind is there, ready to paint the

most colorful (and sensual) mental pictures imaginable. We can never get completely away from temptation.

2. *Temptation is never prompted by God.* He says this clearly in verse 13. He neither is tempted by evil nor does He tempt another. He is holy, remember. Infinitely pure. Totally separate from sin. The next time you find yourself ready to implicate God in your struggle with sensuality, don't waste your time. You have been "carried away" and "enticed" by your *own* lust. It's like those bank robberies we've read about—it's always an "inside job." You'll have to take the rap because you alone are responsible. Verse 14 makes that painfully clear.

3. *Lust always follows the same process.* As you read verses 14 and 15, it is not difficult to see the downward spiral:

Step 1: The bait is dropped.

Step 2: Your inner desire (lust) is attracted to that bait.

Step 3: As you yield, sin occurs. It happens when you bite the bait.

Step 4: Tragic consequences are set in motion. Like the hooked fish, we end up fried.

James 1:13–16 provides us with this thought: *Wake up! Realize that yielding to lust always results in tragic consequences.* This passage takes the fun 'n' games out of sexual temptation.

I find it extremely significant that the Greek term translated "entice" in verse 14 is a fishing term. It means "to lure by a bait." Anybody who's done much fishing quickly gets the picture. In order to attract the fish, the right lure is needed, with just the right eye-catching color or shape or sparkle. And it must be handled just the right way in order for the fish to be "lured" out of his safe hiding place. The more skilled and experienced the angler, the greater his success.

So it is in life. Our enemy, crafty and clever and experienced as he is, knows which lure best attracts each one of us. Our unique inner "itch" longs to be satisfied by that particular outer "scratch." And unless we draw upon the all-conquering power of Christ, unless we consciously apply the same biblical techniques Joseph applied, we'll yield. We'll bite the bait, and we'll suffer the horrible consequences.

Small wonder James ends his counsel with the warning: "Do not be deceived."

Let's lock into our minds these wise words:

Matthew 4:1–11 . . . . . . Use the memorized Word of God. Quote it aloud. Openly wield the sword before the enemy.

1 Corinthians 10:13 . . . . You are not alone. Call out for help and the Lord Jesus Christ will help you endure and escape.

James 1:13–16 . . . . . . Don't be deceived. The bait will inevitably drop. Don't yield. If you do, you will experience tragic consequences. If you refuse, you will remain secure and safe.

As I stated earlier, God will reward your every act of moral restraint.

TAKE CHARGE OF YOUR THOUGHTS!

My Christian friend, let me level with you. You and I are surrounded by a continual stream of sexually suggestive stimuli: advertisements, magazines, novels, soap operas, prime-time television, videos, the film industry, and many of the new fashions and fads. Even much that falls within the category of "the arts" appeals to our sensuous appetites. Obviously, we are not called to clean up our world, but to be salt in it, to shine the light within it.

Salt loses its bite and light becomes dim when we allow these stimuli to hold our attention and find lodging in our minds. The longer this continues to be tolerated, the less discriminating we remain and the less self-control we retain. Silently and slowly, our moral fiber erodes, leaving us an easy prey to the subtle lure of lust. Like pounding ocean waves that finally wear smooth the sharp edges of huge seawall boulders, the endless assault takes a terrible toll on our internal standards. And if allowed to penetrate deeper and deeper, these alien thoughts will find refuge within us, dulling the once-keen edge of our spiritual sensitivity.

On the authority of God's Word, I warn you: *Take charge of your thoughts!* Be extremely careful about what you allow your eyes to observe and your ears to absorb. Ask the Spirit of God to assist you as you apply a filter to everything that enters your mind. Trust Him to provide you with the discipline and discernment you will need. And take it one day at a time. If the Lord could give Joseph the strength he needed to withstand the sensual assault of a woman centuries ago, He will do the same for you today.

Take charge of your thoughts, I repeat. If you do not, I can assure you it will be only a matter of time before you fall, a piece of soft putty in the hands of lust. God offers a better way, the only way to live victoriously:

> . . . *walk by the Spirit, and you will not carry out the desire of the flesh (Galatians 5:16).*

Holy God,

Ours is a world bent on evil and wholly committed to sensuous gratification. We are an "eat, drink, and be merry" society, thinking only of today's pleasures rather than tomorrow's pain.

It is easy to embrace that lifestyle. Even though our conscience tells us otherwise, we are often attracted to the things that offer us immediate satisfaction regardless of the consequences. How hard it is to say no when lust keeps screaming yes!

But when we read of a man like Joseph, our hope is renewed. Our faith is strengthened. Thank You for preserving the record of his life. Grant to us that kind of moral purity. Give us the ability to see beyond the brief excitement sin affords. And may Your Spirit rush in like a flood, reinforcing our decision to resist with immediate, overcoming power. Keep our salt strong and our light bright, O Lord.

In the omnipotent name of Jesus,

Amen.

CHAPTER SEVEN

A SPECIAL WORD FOR WOMEN

Among the stressful issues of the last two decades, the subject of the woman's role in society would certainly rank in the top ten.

All the issues on this subject are much too volatile, extensive, and complicated to be solved in a single chapter less than twenty pages long. I think, for example, of the numerous special concerns of single women, of working moms, of full-time homemakers. In no way am I interested in attempting to address or answer all the questions. You should know that up front before reading any further. That's not the point here.

I am a student and teacher of Scripture and by no means an authority on women. I am a happily married husband of one wife (for almost forty years), strongly supported and deeply loved. I have no hidden frustration I need to "work through" or some secret message all the world desperately needs to hear. I see wrongs that need to be corrected at both extremes and some long overdue rights that need to be declared when the issues are brought into proper focus. My exposure to the problems has been limited, but my eyes have not been closed to the things I've observed, experienced, heard, and read during over thirty years of ministry alongside people, many of whom live in the grays somewhere between bewilderment and deep depression.

I do have one major message I hope to communicate, however. Because it is clearly in need of being proclaimed, and because it is so obviously set forth in God's Word, the Bible, I am able to write about it

123

with a great deal of conviction and certainty. It is this, plain and simple: Women are people of worth and dignity. I sincerely hope those seven words will come through loud and clear as you weave your way through this chapter.

If you are a woman who is beginning to doubt your value, finding yourself in need of encouragement and affirmation, or if you are a man who tends to relegate women, in general, to a subhuman role (and deep down inside you are honestly starting to wonder if that kind of thinking is more traditional than scriptural), then these pages should help.

Extremes fuel the fire of every moment. Push them far enough, scream them loud and long enough, and you've got a revolution on your hands.

Observe . . .

"Never believe a woman, not even a dead one" (Old German proverb).

"Woman is a calamity, but every house must have its curse" (Persian saying).

"Do not trust a good woman, and keep away from a bad one" (Portuguese proverb).

"Wives should be kept barefoot in the summer and pregnant in the winter" (Old Deep South philosophy).

"Men become older, but they never become good" (Oscar Wilde).

"The libido of the American man is focused almost entirely upon his business so that as a husband he is glad to have no responsibilities. . . . It is what I call the laziness of the American man" (Carl Jung).

"I'm loud, and I'm vulgar, and I wear the pants in this house because somebody's got to . . ." (Line from "Who's Afraid of Virginia Woolf?").

"If independence is a necessary concomitant of freedom, women must not marry" (*The Female Eunuch*, Germaine Greer).
"The world will not change . . . liberation will not happen unless individual women agree to be outcasts, eccentrics, perverts, and whatever the powers-to-be choose to call them" (Greer).

Those are extreme statements made by men and women alike, with both sexes representing both sides. So-called authorities shout their wares from free-speech platforms, bestselling books, radio and television talk shows, magazines, and movies. While some are subtle, many are overt and brash. They are "experts" playing Pied Piper roles, each extreme with followers by the thousands.

"Whom do I believe? Which do I follow?"

Well, there's the "total" woman advocate saying true femininity means "full surrender to your man." But there's also the radical feminist and her ilk who sneer at such "subservient advice," speaking more of absolute equality, female dominance, and assertiveness. Both have success stories to bolster their public image. Both claim a philosophy that works, one that offers answers to the woman who lingers somewhere between feeling forgotten and being frustrated.

DIRTY DEALS, INDEPENDENCE, SUBMISSION, AND OTHER TOPICS

Not being a woman, I am unable to enter into a soul-level struggle with such warlike propaganda. But I have had opportunity to observe the field of battle and do a little analysis of the situation. Here are some of my observations:

1. *Some women today have gotten a dirty deal and have every reason to be angry.*

Wife-battering is, for some husbands, a favorite indoor sport. Emotional cruelty and abuse is just as damaging—and far more prevalent than physical mistreatment. Many a fine, faithful wife and mother has been abandoned to make it on her own. She has several small children and no marketable skills. Adding insult to injury, she helped her now-runaway husband through school.

2. *Some women lack discernment and clear thinking on today's propaganda from both extremes.*

Those who have been ripped off are ready-made shock troops for the feminist movement. What's there to question? She's been shoved down and stomped on long enough, and anybody who's willing to champion her cause gets her vote.

Then there's the "traditional woman" who lived with a dominant dad and a mousy mom, was raised in a culture that frequently tightened the screws on submission—far beyond the biblical bounds—and who (naturally) married a guy who wanted a doormat for a wife. She's as gullible to those who demand absolute silence and total submission as her aggressive sister is to the message of the militant feminist.

3. *As a result, some women have become much more masculine than feminine, unattractively independent, and offensively assertive.*

This seems to come with the territory. Whoever buys the line wears the garb. I know of few things more disgusting, personally, or more fallacious, biblically, than a lovely, feminine, once-attractive lady who has adopted masculine responses and characteristics.

4. *On the other hand, some women have begun to blend into the woodwork, mistaking submission as a synonym for spinelessness, passivity, human bondage, and waiting on every whim of her man, with no will of her own.*

If you have ever witnessed a lady with this mentality, you've seen a pathetic sight. It's what I call the "whipped dog" look. More often than not, she lives with a frightfully low self-image, wearing an inferior look that announces incompetence, timidity, and fear. To make matters worse, this person frequently lives under the delusion that she is modeling the biblical message. Few things could be further from the truth!

5. *Confusion often reigns when it comes to knowing a woman's role and identity according to the Scriptures.*

I write that with a sigh, not a frown. It's understandable, since women have so many voices of authority to choose from, each inviting, "Follow me." And so? So they roam from seminar to seminar, conference to congress, book to film series to cassette tape, hoping to find a guru who will solve that gnawing dilemma.

6. *In our society today, only a few are genuinely satisfied and fulfilled, whether married or single.*

Have you ever known a time when more people are less happy? How many do you know who live with someone whom they deeply love, are secure enough to have nothing to prove, enjoy living, and absorb affirmation and security in their home? Precious few. The result is a devastating blow on today's family. You may be considered somewhat weird if you're happily married (or happily single), enjoy children, and appreciate and uphold things like sexual fidelity, long-term commitments, and other facets of the wedding vows.

DRIVEN TOWARD TWO EXTREMES

I could go on, but we need no further evidence. Small wonder more women aren't confused—or eaten alive by the stress of competing voices and demands. In summary, two extremes have boarded the ship of today's society.

First, there is the overly aggressive woman who is unwilling to be led or reproved by almost anyone, especially a man, and who hates terms like "submit" or "the woman's place." This person leaves in her wake threatened husband(s), confused and insecure kids, loneliness, isolation, and a variety of offenses.

Second, there is the inordinately passive, intimidated woman who lacks confidence and charm, opinions and convictions. She is not simply committed to her home, she's *bound* there. The thought of working outside the home is foreign to this lady. She is therefore fairly unaware of the real world beyond her walls, for she is slavishly at the disposal of her husband and children, cowering and apologetic, forever waiting to fill no role above that of a silent servant. I find that this type of woman suffers most disorientation when (a) the children leave the nest, and/or (b) the husband dies prematurely and she is forced to face the blast of hard, cold reality.

The first extreme represents what we might call a secular philosophy of life, the second, a traditional philosophy. Neither, allow me to repeat, is appealing or biblical. Only a casual reading of several scriptural passages (for example, Proverbs 31, the most detailed and lengthy portrait of a woman in all the Bible) will reveal that neither extreme is found in God's Word . . . unless, of course, the reader reads it into the text.

WHAT HAS CAUSED SUCH EXTREMES?

As we look at these extremes, a question emerges: Why have we moved in these directions? What are the causes of such biblically inaccurate and emotionally unhealthy extremes? I can think of several causes.

1. *A misunderstanding and misapplication of "submission."*

Husbands and wives alike have done this. Pastors and other so-called authorities have also contributed to this most unfortunate problem.

2. *A failure on the part of Christian husbands to carry out three essential responsibilities, namely:*

- to think biblically,
- to lead fairly,
- to release unselfishly.

3. *A strong, well-organized action from the secular world system to "liberate" today's woman . . . regardless.*

Even those who don't want to be "liberated" are made to appear foolish and backward. The fulfilled woman who enjoys being at home is mocked by the system.

4. *An equally strong resistance from some voices in Christendom to keep the Christian woman boxed in, seated, and silent.*

HOW DOES SCRIPTURE PORTRAY WOMEN?

Perhaps it's at this point that we need to spend some time. If the Bible does not portray an extreme picture of women, what picture does it provide?

I decided to answer that question several years ago. With pencil and paper in hand, I began to turn through the pages of the Bible and take a close, firsthand look at many of the women found there. By the time I came to the final pages, I was struck with one overriding thought. Except in a few isolated and special occasions, the women who appear in Scripture are competent, secure, qualified people who had responsible roles to fill. In so doing, these women played a vital part in the shaping of history and in the development of lives. They are beautiful examples of humanity at every economic level of society.

Let me share with you some of the examples I found in my study. But let's limit them to the New Testament and to just a few of the more prominent cases.

- Mary and Martha were close friends of Jesus (Luke 10:38–39).
- Mary anointed Jesus prior to His death (John 12:3).
- Many women lamented Jesus' crucifixion (Luke 23:27–31; John 19:25).
- Women visited Jesus' tomb on resurrection morning (Luke 23:55–24:1).
- Early church leaders responded positively to widows' complaints (Acts 6:1–7).
- Dorcas abounded "with deeds of kindness and charity" and was extremely well known in her community (Acts 9:36).
- The church gathered in Mary's home to pray for Peter (Acts 12:12).
- Jews aroused "the devout women of prominence" against Paul and Barnabas (Acts 13:50).
- Women gathered for worship at Philippi. Paul spoke to them (Acts 16:13).
- Lydia was a successful businesswoman who became a Christian and prevailed upon Paul and his colleagues to meet in her home (Acts 16:14–15).
- In Thessalonica, "a number of the leading women" were responsive to Paul's and Silas's teaching (Acts 17:4).
- In Berea, "many . . . believed, along with a number of prominent Greek women . . ." (Acts 17:12).
- In Athens, some believed, including a woman named Damaris (Acts 17:34).

- Aquila and his wife, Priscilla, were often mentioned (Acts 18:2, 18).
- Paul called these two his "fellow workers" (Romans 16:3).
- Both Aquila and Priscilla helped hone Apollos's theology (Acts 18:26).
- Paul mentioned Phoebe as "a servant of the church . . . helper of many, and of myself as well" (Romans 16:1–2).
- "Chloe's people" gave Paul information on a Corinthian problem (1 Corinthians 1:11).
- Widows were given special attention, assistance, and care (1 Timothy 5:3–16).
- Older women were instructed to "encourage" younger women (Titus 2:4).
- Apphia was called "our sister" in the Philemon letter (Philemon 2).
- The second letter of John was addressed to "the chosen lady . . ." (2 John 1).

Even in this limited and random list, you can see numerous accounts of significant women who occupied places and roles of strategic importance. This underscores that God never intended the woman to feel inferior or to live fearfully beneath some heavy cloud of unfair domination. While no one who takes Scripture seriously can deny that a wife must, indeed, fit into her husband's plans (1 Peter 3:1) and ultimately allow him the place of final authority in the home (Ephesians 5:22), in no way is she ever viewed as an individual lacking in worth or dignity. Look back over that list and decide for yourself.

Perhaps you have begun to catch a rather bold implication in my comments. The word is *balance*. In my opinion, this is one of the clearest marks of maturity a Christian woman can demonstrate today . . . living apart from either extreme, yet fully alive; functioning to her maximum capacity; free to be who she is, yet willing to live within the God-given limits He has prescribed for the home. She doesn't chafe at being a help and an encouragement to her husband. She has few frustrations (aside from those normal to all humanity!) connected with her place in life or her contributions to her world, which is broader, by the way, than the fence surrounding her place of residence.

A BRIEF WORD TO HUSBANDS

I sense that some women who read these lines are thinking, *Talk to my husband. That balanced role you describe is very appealing to me—something I long for—but he can't see it. He's holding me down. I'm not a rebel, but I see the need for broadening my world and finding areas where my self-esteem can be strengthened.*

Husband, can you take it straight? I believe you can. You need to take an honest, realistic look at your wife. You also need to hear what she's saying. And why she is saying it. You would do well to imagine yourself in her place for a change (which includes living with you, pal!). Visualize yourself trying to find meaning and purpose in the limited space her responsibilities require of her. Imagine trying to respond to *your* expectations and demands.

How about a weekend away, just the two of you? How about a long talk? How about soon? Here are a few discussion questions to get the conversation flowing:

- What are some of the things you'd love to do—or become—as a woman that seem impossible right now? Please be specific and open with me.
- Am I sensitive to your deep needs? Are there areas where I could improve and give you renewed hope as my wife?
- I want to demonstrate true love to you and to be God's man in our home. In your opinion, is my love freeing or smothering? Am I allowing you room and time to become the woman God would have you to be?
- Love and commitment deepen as two people work toward common goals in a marriage. Let's talk about our goals as husband and wife.
- If something suddenly happened to me, how would you be able to go on? Are we being realistic with inevitable things that will impact our future, like the children leaving home or my dying prematurely?

- What are some of your fears? Your hurts? Your frustrations?
- Ever think about walking away from it all? What things can I do to help strengthen your commitment to me and to our marriage?
- On a scale of one to ten (one being the lowest, ten the highest), how would you rank our relationship? Why?

Now, friend, those are gutsy, let's-not-skate-around-the-block questions. But if you are willing to take that risk and to give your wife the freedom to express herself in those areas (without your becoming angry or defensive), you won't have much trouble knowing the whole truth concerning your marriage. You'll also gain some valuable insights into why things have become so strained under the roof where you live.

Is this kind of thing biblical? Is it part of being a loving husband? Look at 1 Peter 3:7:

> *You husbands likewise, live with your wives in an understanding way, as with a weaker vessel, since she is a woman; and grant her honor as a fellow heir of the grace of life, so that your prayers may not be hindered.*

Study those words carefully. Read them again in another rendering:

> *In the same way you married men should live considerately with [your wives], with an intelligent recognition [of the marriage relation], honoring the woman as [physically] the weaker, but [realizing that you] are joint heirs of the grace (God's unmerited favor) of life, in order that your prayers may not be hindered and cut off.—Otherwise you cannot pray effectively. (The Amplified Bible).*

Peter's advice could be summarized in three short statements: dwell with your wife; know the woman you live with; give her honor. He's not simply saying eat, sleep, dress, work around the house, and entertain together. He's saying *be* together. Intimately aware and acquainted. Get to know that lady! Discover her. Treat her with respect. Assign her honor. Let me urge you to follow through with your responsibilities before you come down any harder on *her* to carry out her part of the relationship. 'Nuff said.

A BALANCED WOMAN OF GOD

Ladies, after my scriptural search, I came to three conclusions regarding this matter of being a balanced woman of God. Each will require a good deal of your time, and each will call for a fair amount of effort if you hope to put it into action personally.

> *A balanced woman of God sees Scripture as God's vital and relevant Word, worth her attention, devotion, and application.*

I learned this principle from Timothy's mother, Eunice, and his maternal grandmother, Lois.

> *And [Paul] came also to Derbe and to Lystra. And behold, a certain disciple was there, named Timothy, the son of a Jewish woman who was a believer, but his father was a Greek, and he was well spoken of by the brethren who were in Lystra and Iconium (Acts 16:1–2).*

> *I [Paul] thank God, whom I serve with a clear conscience the way my forefathers did, as I constantly remember you [Timothy] in my prayers night and day, longing to see you, even as I recall your tears, so that I may be filled with joy. For I am mindful of the sincere faith within you, which first dwelt in your grandmother Lois, and your mother Eunice, and I am sure that it is in you as well (2 Timothy 1:3–5).*

> *And that from childhood you have known the sacred writings which are able to give you the wisdom that leads to salvation through faith which is in Christ Jesus (2 Timothy 3:15).*

On the basis of these biblical examples, I challenge you to get serious about the Bible. Start meeting with God on a regular basis each day. Don't sacrifice time spent in your Bible for hours consumed with magazines, novels, TV, and listening to the gossip garbage from neighbors! Become a woman of the Word. You'll be amazed at the built-in filter system God's truth will provide.

A balanced woman of God sees herself as valuable, gifted, responsible for her own growth and maturity . . . not overly dependent on anyone to get her through life or to make her secure.

I learned this second principle from a first-century business-woman named Lydia and from the wife of Aquila, a terrific lady named Priscilla.

Therefore putting out to sea from Troas, we ran a straight course to Samothrace, and on the day following to Neapolis; and from there to Philippi, which is a leading city of the district of Macedonia, a Roman colony; and we were staying in this city for some days. And on the Sabbath day we went outside the gate to a riverside, where we were supposing that there would be a place of prayer; and we sat down and began speaking to the women who had assembled. And a certain woman named Lydia, from the city of Thyatira, a seller of purple fabrics, a worshiper of God, was listening; and the Lord opened her heart to respond to the things spoken by Paul. And when she and her household had been baptized, she urged us, saying, "If you have judged me to be faithful to the Lord, come into my house and stay." And she prevailed upon us (Acts 16:11–15).

After these things [Paul] left Athens and went to Corinth. And he found a certain Jew named Aquila, a native of Pontus, having recently come from Italy with his wife Priscilla, because Claudius had commanded all the Jews to leave Rome. He came to them, and because he was of the same trade, he stayed with them and they were working; for by trade they were tent-makers. . . .

And Paul, having remained many days longer, took leave of the brethren and put out to sea for Syria, and with him were Priscilla and Aquila (Acts 18:1–3, 18; see also Romans 16:3).

Both of these women were extremely competent people; persuasive and responsible, yet teachable and gracious. Again, there was balance. And both were keen thinkers. Priscilla joined her husband as they both (!) helped correct Apollos who was soft in one particular area of his theology.

> *Now a certain Jew named Apollos, an Alexandrian by birth, an eloquent man, came to Ephesus; and he was mighty in the Scriptures. This man had been instructed in the way of the Lord; and being fervent in spirit, he was speaking and teaching accurately the things concerning Jesus, being acquainted only with the baptism of John; and he began to speak out boldly in the synagogue. But when Priscilla and Aquila heard him, they took him aside and explained to him the way of God more accurately. And when he wanted to go across to Achaia, the brethren encouraged him and wrote to the disciples to welcome him; and when he had arrived, he helped greatly those who had believed through grace; for he powerfully refuted the Jews in public, demonstrating by the Scriptures that Jesus was the Christ (Acts 18:24–28).*

I'm not saying that these women left their husbands (if Lydia was married) to "do their thing," but they were both highly respected by the apostle Paul. I'm confident Apollos was equally impressed.

Lady, stop blaming someone else for your lack of growth! And remember that even though you are joined to your husband as "heirs together," you're not Siamese twins! If you need your husband for security and hope to go on, it's possible you have assigned him a role only your Lord should fill. Think about that.

> *A balanced woman of God sees the Lord as her strength, her refuge, and her shield when things refuse to be resolved.*

I could be tempted to end this chapter like a fairy tale, promising you that all your stress fractures will be mended, that

life will suddenly start changing, that your husband will become
all you need during the next seventy-two hours, or that your world
will begin to blossom like the rose next spring. I refuse to yield to
that temptation.

The fact is, you and I know that usually *we* must change
before anyone else will . . . and even then there's no guarantee. You
may live with a very strong-willed man. He may not be willing to
talk about it anymore (you've tried, haven't you?), to say nothing
of reading some chapter in a book written by a guy he doesn't know
(who lives in California, no less!).

Well, take hope. In Acts 21:7–14 a group of people (several
of them women) had difficulty convincing a strong man to change
his mind. In fact, they failed to do so. But rather than fighting and
forcing, they said simply, "The will of the Lord be done!" (v. 14),
and they left the results with God.

You may need that counsel most of all today. Please—do not
rely on emotional manipulation or sexual bargaining or threats of
leaving. This is a case for God to handle. "The will of the Lord be
done!" The world says, "Don't be stupid—pull out. Get even. Fight
back. You've come a long way, baby. *Don't give in!* It's high time
that men learned you're NOT GOING TO TAKE IT ANY
LONGER!"

But if you wish to be a balanced woman of God (one of the
world's endangered species), you will resist that advice. You'll
remember that the Lord your God points to an alternate route
which, by the way, is despised and mocked in the feminist movement. But of far greater importance, it is clearly set forth in the
pages of His ageless Book.

The alternate counsel? God urges you to hang in there
(except in cases of physical abuse or danger) and let Him work on
your behalf. He urges you to trust in Him and not panic. To stay
close to Him and allow Him to sustain you and nourish you and be
your stability; your thick, comforting shield of protection. He
offers you the ability to hold up even when the stress and pressure
don't go away.

My friend, it is essential that you believe what these pages
have been saying. Believe this statement, even though you may not

be hearing it from those who live with you in the same house: You are a person of worth and dignity. The word is *valuable*. You are too valuable for your Savior and Lord to let go of you. He does not expect you to right all the wrongs, or to fight your own battles. You've tried too many times already, remember? Now it's time to rely with calm assurance on His all-conquering power. Do that, starting this very moment.

May the Lord our God give you these three things: Great grace to endure without fear, genuine mercy to forgive without resentment, and prevailing peace to continue without doubt.

Dear Father,

How difficult it is to trust You during times of trouble. This problem is magnified when many authoritative voices are telling us not to do this or to start doing that, all of which is counter to Your counsel. But they are close by and You, Lord, seem so far away at times . . . so slow to work . . . so terribly silent.

Being a woman pulled in various directions is hard enough when things run smoothly. But it gets downright frightening when relationships are strained and our emotions within start screaming for attention. You know how we are, Lord! It seems like everything works against our feeling that we're worthwhile, valuable people. Our heads tell us, "Yes," but our hearts often say, "No."

We really want to do what's right. Deep within, our greatest desire is to obey Your voice, to walk within the parameters of Your perfect will, even if that means we don't get our way or we can't understand Your plan. It's easy at such times, however, for us to allow fear to come in like the morning frost and blight our faith. When that happens, we run to extremes and act immaturely rather than stand firmly within the safe and godly boundaries of balance. We need Your help, Father.

Do give us new measures of grace. And a vast amount of mercy. And Your matchless peace. May those special gifts free us from panic and get us in tune with Your Word so that everything false and phony will be filtered out as discernment replaces gullibility. May all this give

*us a maturity that restrains us from embracing error clothed deceitfully
in the garb of truth. With quiet confidence, we trust You.*

    In the name of Jesus,
    Amen.

PART TWO

SPIRITUAL THERAPY

CHAPTER EIGHT

LEISURE

This chapter has one primary objective: to help you enjoy yourself, your life, and your Lord more . . . without feeling guilty or unspiritual. Yes, enjoy!

In our work-worshiping society, that is no small task. Many have cultivated such an unrealistic standard of high-level achievement that a neurotic compulsion to perform, to produce, to accomplish the maximum is now the rule rather than the exception. Enough is no longer enough.

Christians are not immune from stress fractures, especially vocational Christian workers. How many pastors or missionaries do you know who truly enjoy guilt-free leisure? How many Christian executives can you name who really take sufficient time to relax? On the other hand, how often have you heard someone boast about not having taken a vacation in several years? Or being too busy to have time to rest and repair?

Work is fast becoming the American Christian's major source of identity. The answer to most of our problems (we are told) is "work harder." And to add the ultimate pressure, "You aren't really serving the Lord unless you consistently push yourself to the point of fatigue." It's the old burn-out-rather-than-rust-out line.

This chapter offers a different rationale. It says not only, "It's okay to relax," but also, "It's essential!" Without encouraging an irresponsible mentality, it says, "You can have fun and still be efficient." In fact, you will be more efficient!

Pussy-cat, pussy-cat, where have you been?
I've been to London to look at the queen.
Pussy-cat, pussy-cat, what did you there?
I frightened a little mouse under the chair.[1]

Now there's a rhyme I'll never understand.
That little pussy-cat had the chance of her lifetime. All of London stretched out before her. Dozens of famous, time-worn scenes to drink in. Westminster Abbey. Trafalgar Square. Ten Downing Street, Churchill's old residence. The unsurpassable British Museum. That old Marble Arch at Hyde Park. She could have scurried up an old lamppost and watched the changing of the guards. Or slipped in the side entrance and enjoyed an evening with the London Philharmonic. Or studied the immortal architecture at St. Paul's Cathedral.

She probably didn't even realize it was the historic Thames rushing by beneath that huge rusty bridge she scampered across, chasing more mice. After all, she didn't even take the time to scope out the queen as Her Majesty walked across the courtyard. Not this cat! She was such a mouseaholic that she couldn't break with the monotonous routine even when she was on vacation. Same old grind . . . even in London. What a bore!

Can you imagine the scene as her husband met her at the plane back in New York?

"Hi, Fluff. How was it? Didja have fun? What did ya see? Tell me all about it."

"Well, Tom, uh, it all started when I went in the first day to see the queen. There was this little mouse under her throne. I darted after it . . . and, well, from then on, Tom, it was just like here. Do you realize how many mice there are in London?"

"You *what?* You mean to tell me you spent ten whole days in London and all you can say for it is this stuff about mice?"

That mouseaholic has a lot to say to all workaholics . . . and churchaholics, for that matter. Overcommitted, pushed, in a hurry, grim-faced, and determined, we plow through our responsibilities like a freight train under a full head of steam. What we lack in enthusiasm, we make up for in diligence. And we ignore the stinging reality that monotony now follows us as closely as our own shadow.

IS FATIGUE NEXT TO GODLINESS?

Strangely, the one thing we need is the last thing we consider. We've been programmed to think that fatigue is next to godliness. That the more exhausted we are (and look!), the more spiritual we are and the more we earn God's smile of approval. We bury all thoughts of enjoying life . . . for we all know that committed, truly committed, Christians are those who work, work, work. Preferably, with great intensity. As a result, we have become a generation of people who worship our work, who work at our play, and who play at our worship.

Hold it! Who wrote that rule? Why have we bought that philosophy? What gave someone the right to declare such a statement?

I challenge you to support it from the Scriptures. Or to go back into the life (and *lifestyle*) of Jesus Christ and find a trace of corroborating evidence that He embraced such a theory. Some will be surprised to learn there is not one reference in the New Testament saying (or even implying) that Jesus intensely worked and labored in an occupation to the point of emotional exhaustion. No, but there are several times when we are told He deliberately took a break. He got away from the demands of the public and enjoyed periods of relaxation with His disciples. I'm not saying He rambled through His ministry in an aimless, halfhearted fashion. Not at all! But neither did He come anywhere near an ulcer. Never once do we find Him in a frenzy.

His was a life of beautiful balance. He accomplished everything the Father sent Him to do. Everything. And He did it without ignoring those essential times of leisure. If that is the way He lived, then it makes good sense for you and me to live that way, too.

THE PERSON TO IMITATE: GOD

Since most humans suffer from a lack of balance in their lives, our best counsel on this subject comes from God's Word. In Paul's letter to the Christians in Ephesus, he includes this most unusual command:

Be imitators of God, therefore, as dearly loved children
. . . (Ephesians 5:1, NIV).

Maybe you never realized such a statement was in the Bible.
It seems unusual: "imitators of God"!

The Greek term translated "be imitators" is *mimeomai*, from
which we get the English word *mimic*. One reliable scholar says
this verb "is always used in exhortations, and always in the continuous tense, suggesting a constant habit or practice."[2]

In other words, this is neither a passing thought nor a once-
in-a-blue-moon experience. The practice of our being people who
"mimic God" is to become our daily habit. We are to do what He
does. Respond to life as He responds. Emulate similar traits. Model
His style.

But to do that, to be an imitator of God, requires that we
come to terms with the value of quietness, slowing down, coming
apart from the noise and speed of today's pace and broadening our
lives with a view of the eternal reach of time. It means saying no to
more and more activities that increase the speed of our squirrel
cage, knowing God requires that we "be still" (Psalm 46:10, NIV).

It means if I'm a cat in London, I do more, much more, than
frighten mice under chairs. Or if I'm a pastor, I do more than tend
the sheep. I must—or I ultimately begin to walk dangerously near
the ragged edge of emotional disintegration. It also means I refuse
to be driven by guilt and unrealistic demands (mine or others). To
be God-mimics, we must begin to realize that leisure is not a take-
it-or-leave-it luxury.

Please understand that leisure is more than idle time not
devoted to paid occupations. Some of the most valuable work done
in the world has been done at leisure . . . and never paid for in cash.
Leisure is free activity. Labor is compulsory activity. In leisure, we
do what we like, but in labor, we do what we must. In our labor, we
meet the objective needs and demands of others—our employer,
the public, people who are affected by and through our work. But
in leisure, we scratch the subjective itches within ourselves. In
leisure, our minds are liberated from the immediate, the necessary.
As we incorporate leisure into the mainstream of our world, we

gain perspective. We lift ourselves above the grit and grind of mere existence.

Interestingly, "leisure" comes from the Latin word *licere*, which means "to be permitted." If we are ever going to inculcate leisure into our otherwise utilitarian routine, we must give ourselves permission to do so.

But this calls for a close look. We need some specific guidelines to focus on that will help us imitate God and at the same time "permit" us to cultivate leisure in our lives.

FOUR GUIDELINES FROM GENESIS

If we are to imitate God as a daily habit of life, we need to nail down some specific guidelines. It occurred to me recently that an excellent place to locate those specifics in the Scriptures would be the first place He reveals Himself to us—the book of Genesis, especially the first two chapters.

If you were to take the time to read this familiar section, you would discover that God is involved in four activities:

- He creates,
- He communicates,
- He rests,
- He relates.

Let's limit our thoughts to those four guidelines. Each one fits perfectly into the cultivation of leisure. They form some excellent guidelines to follow as we begin to develop an accurate concept of leisure.

CREATIVITY-PENS TO PAINT BRUSHES TO PATIOS

First and foremost, God is engaged in the act of creation, according to Genesis 1 and 2. He begins with that which is "formless and void" (1:2), lacking meaning, beauty, and purpose.

He takes time to create with His own hands. In His mind were thoughts of a universe, indescribably beautiful. He mentally pictured vast expanses of land masses, deep oceans, colorful vegetation, an almost endless variety of living creatures . . . not to mention the stars, the planets, and the perfect motion of all. Finally,

He creates mankind with a body and mind that still amazes students of physiology and psychology.

As He created, He added the music, harmony, and rhythm of movement—the miracle of birth and growth, the full spectrum of colors, sights, and sounds. He cared about details—from snowflakes to butterfly wings, from pansy petals to the bones of bodies, from the microscopic world of biology to the telescopic world of astronomy.

In doing all this, He set the pace. He, the first to create, announced its significance.

If I may suddenly jump forward to today, let me ask a penetrating question: Are you taking time to create? Obviously, you cannot create a solar system or bring forth an ocean from nothing, but you can make things with your hands. You can write things with your pen . . . or paint things with your brush . . . or compose things, using your piano or guitar or harmonica. You can dream things with your mind and then try to invent them or draw them or in other ways bring them to reality through some creative process.

You hold a book in your hand. There was a time when this particular chapter you are reading did not exist. It began as a dream, an idea which came to me, by the way, in one of my leisure moments. I gave myself permission to relax for several days on vacation, and this chapter is the ultimate result of that occasion. Its words have not been copied, nor does the flow of thought emerge from some required or forced structure. It has been a creative experience. One of my most enjoyable leisure activities is writing—something I would never have thought possible twenty years ago. But now I realize I've had this itch inside me most of my life. It wasn't until I began to let it out freely and fully that a whole new dimension of my life was added. And it's such fun!

All children have built-in creativity. Just look at the things they make and do (and say!) on their own. There is an enormous wealth of creative powers in the mind of a child. Walt Disney believed that and often spoke of it. But if we aren't careful, we adults will squelch it. We'll fail to encourage it or cultivate it or even let it out of its cage. Why? Well, it takes a little extra time and it often costs some money. I should add that it tends to be messy. Not many really creative people—in the process of creating—keep everything neat, picked up, and in its place.

There's a good motto to remember if you're determined to encourage and cultivate creativity:

A creative mess . . . is better than tidy idleness.

If we are going to imitate God, we'll need to find creative outlets in times of leisure. Yours may be music or one of the arts. It may be in the area of interior design. My wife enjoys house plants and quilting. You may enjoy gardening or landscaping projects, woodworking, or brick and stone work around the house. We had our patio enclosed during the remodeling of our house. Both the bricklayer and the carpenter we used employed a great deal of creativity in their skills. It's an added plus when you can create and even get paid for it! But regardless, our creativity needs expression.

COMMUNICATION—TO SELF AND TO OTHERS

If you read the Genesis account of creation rather carefully, you'll see that interspersed within the creative week were times of communication. God made things, then said, "That's good." After the sixth day, His evaluation increased to, "That's very good."

The Godhead communicated prior to the creation of man, you may recall.

Then God said, "Let Us make man in Our image, according to Our likeness; and let them rule over the fish of the sea and over the birds of the sky and over the cattle and over all the earth, and over every creeping thing that creeps on the earth" (Genesis 1:26).

And *after* creating man, He communicated with him, the highest form of life He had made.

And God blessed them; and God said to them, "Be fruitful and multiply, and fill the earth, and subdue it; and rule over the fish of the sea and over the birds of the sky, and over every living thing that moves on the earth." Then God said,

"Behold, I have given you every plant yielding seed that is on the surface of all the earth, and every tree which has fruit yielding seed; it shall be food for you; and to every beast of the earth and to every bird of the sky and to every thing that moves on the earth which has life, I have given every green plant for food"; and it was so (Genesis 1:28–30).

Again, I'd like to apply this to our times. Initially, in leisure, we take time to communicate with ourselves (as God did) and affirm ourselves, "That's good . . . that's very good." Do you do that? Most of us are good at criticizing ourselves and finding fault with what we have done or failed to do. I'd like to suggest an alternate plan—spend some leisure finding pleasure and satisfaction in what you have done as well as in who and what you are. Sound too liberal? Why? Since when is a good self-esteem liberal?

There are times we need to tell ourselves, "Good job!" when we know that is true. I smile as I write this to you, but I must confess that occasionally I even say to myself, "That's *very* good, Swindoll," when I am pleased with something I've done. That isn't conceited pride, my friend. It's acknowledging in words the feelings of the heart. The Lord knows that we hear more than enough internal putdowns! Communicating in times of leisure includes self-affirmation, acknowledging, of course, that God ultimately gets the glory. After all, He's the One who makes it all possible.

Leisure also includes times of communicating with others who are important to us, just as God the Creator did with man the creature. Unless we are careful, the speed of our lives will reduce our communication to grunts, frowns, stares, and unspoken assumptions. Be honest. Has that begun to happen? Sometimes our children mirror the truth of our pace.

I vividly remember some time back being caught in the undertow of too many commitments in too few days. It wasn't long before I was snapping at my wife and our children, choking down my food at mealtimes, and feeling irritated at those unexpected interruptions through the day. Before long, things around our home started reflecting the pattern of my hurry-up style. It was becoming unbearable.

I distinctly recall after supper one evening the words of our younger daughter, Colleen. She wanted to tell me about something important that had happened to her at school that day. She hurriedly began, "Daddy-I-wanna-tell-you-somethin'-and-I'll-tell-you-really-fast."

Suddenly realizing her frustration, I answered, "Honey, you can tell me . . . and you don't have to tell me really fast. Say it slowly."

I'll never forget her answer: "Then listen slowly."

I had taken no time for leisure. Not even at meals with my family. Everything was uptight. And guess what began to break down? You're right, those all-important communication lines.

God not only made man. He talked with him, He listened to him. He considered His creature valuable enough to spend time with, to respond to. It took time, but He believed it was justified.

There are entire books written on communication, so I'll not be so foolish as to think I can develop the subject adequately here. I only want to emphasize its importance. It is imperative that we understand that without adding sufficient leisure time to our schedule for meaningful communication, a relationship with those who are important to us will disintegrate faster than we can keep it in repair.

Take time to listen, to feel, to respond. In doing so, we "imitate God" in our leisure.

REST TIME!

Following the sixth day of creation, the Lord God deliberately stopped working.

> *Thus the heavens and the earth were completed, and all their hosts. And by the seventh day God completed His work which He had done; and He rested on the seventh day from all His work which He had done. Then God blessed the seventh day and sanctified it, because in it He rested from all His work which God had created and made (Genesis 2:1–3).*

He rested. Take special note of that. It wasn't that there was nothing else He could have done. It certainly wasn't because He was exhausted. Omnipotence never gets tired! He hadn't run out of ideas, for omniscience knows no mental limitations. He could easily have made more worlds, created an infinite number of other forms of life, and provided multiple millions of galaxies beyond what He did.

But He didn't. He stopped.

He spent an entire day resting. In fact, He "blessed the seventh day and sanctified it," something He did not do on the other six days. He marked this one day off as extremely special. Like none other. Sounds to me like He made the day on which He rested a "priority" period of time.

If we intend to "imitate God," we, too, will need to make rest a priority.

- A good night's rest on a regular basis,
- A full day's rest at least once a week,
- Moments of rest snatched here and there during the week,
- Vacation times of rest for the refreshment and repair of both body and soul,
- A release from the fierce grip of intense stress brought on by daily hassles.

Several things contribute to our lack of inner rest:

- A poorly developed sense of humor;
- Focusing more on what we don't have rather than on what we do have;
- Failure to give play, fun, rest, and leisure a proper place of dignity;
- Our strong tendency to compete and compare, leading to a wholesale dissatisfaction with things as they are;
- Preoccupation with always wanting more;
- Self-imposed guilt . . . unrealistic expectations;
- Long-time "heredity habit" of the all-work-and-no-play-will-make-me-happy philosophy of life.

The result? Look around. Stretched across most faces of Americans driving to and from work is boredom. Not fulfillment.

Not a deep sense of satisfaction. Not even a smile of quiet contentment.

Even though our work-week is decreasing and our weekend time is increasing, our country lacks inner peace. External leisure does not guarantee internal rest, does it?

For sure, our nation believes in the theory of leisure. I heard over a television documentary that we spend more on recreation each year than we do on education, construction of new homes, or national defense! Yet for all that, mental hospitals remain overcrowded . . . and most of the patients are not what we would call senior citizens.

Time on our hands, we have. But meaningful "rest" in the biblical sense of the term? No way!

I suggest you and I do more than cluck our tongues and wag our heads at the problem. That helps nobody! Our greatest contribution to the answer is a radical break with the rut of normal living. My good friend, Tim Hansel of Summit Expeditions, suggests taking different kinds of vacations: midget vacations or minivacations (two minutes or more!) or, if you're able, maxivacations . . . or even, if possible, super-maxi-vacations where you take time to enjoy extended leisure, calling that year the "Year of Adventure" where we try our hand at sailing, rock climbing, skydiving, karate—or whatever.

Change your routine, my friend. Blow the dust of boredom off your schedule. Shake yourself loose and get a taste of fresh life. Need several suggestions to add "zip" to your leisure?

- Begin jogging and/or an exercise program;
- Buy a bicycle and start pedaling two or three miles each day;
- Get a CD of your favorite music and lie down flat on your back, drinking in the sounds;
- Enroll in a local class and take a stab at painting;
- Start writing letters of encouragement to people you appreciate;
- Make something out of wood with your own hands;

- Dig around in the soil, plant a small garden, and watch God cooperate with your efforts;
- Take a gourmet cooking class;
- Spend some time at the library and pick up several good books on subjects or people of interest to you . . . then sit back, munch on an apple, and read, read, read;
- Plan a camping or backpacking trip soon with one of your children, your mate, or a friend, and spend a night or two out under the stars;
- Pull out all those old snapshots, sort them, and put them into albums;
- Write some poetry;
- Visit a museum or zoo in your area;
- By the way, don't miss those sunrises and sunsets, or the smells along with the sights.

Broaden your world. Kick away the thick, brick walls of tradition. Silence the old enemy Guilt, who will sing his same old tune in your ears. And work on that deep crease between your eyes. Look for things to laugh at . . . and *laugh out loud*. It's biblical! "A joyful heart is good medicine, but a broken spirit dries up the bones" (Proverbs 17:22).

Comedian Bill Cosby is right. There's a smile down inside of you that's just dying to come out! It won't until you give yourself permission. Rest releases humor.

One more glance at the Genesis passage will be worth our effort. Remember where we've been?

- God created . . . in leisure; so do *we*.
- God communicated . . . in leisure; so must *we*.

But He also *related* with the man and woman He made.

RELATING—WITH OUR FRIENDS

The passage in Genesis 2 is so familiar. After God made man, He observed a need inside that life, a nagging loneliness that Adam couldn't shake.

> *Then the LORD God said, "It is not good for the man to*
> *be alone; I will make him a helper suitable for him" (Genesis*
> *2:18).*

As a fulfillment to the promise to help Adam with his need for companionship, God got involved:

> *So the LORD God caused a deep sleep to fall upon the*
> *man, and he slept; then He took one of his ribs, and closed up*
> *the flesh at that place. And the LORD God fashioned into a*
> *woman the rib which He had taken from the man, and*
> *brought her to the man (Genesis 2:21–22).*

Later we read that the Lord came to relate to His creatures "in the cool of the day" (Genesis 3:8). I take it that such a time must have been a common practice between the Lord God and Adam and Eve.

He considered them valuable, so the infinite Creator-God took time to relate with His friends in the Garden of Eden. He got personally involved. He observed their needs. He carved out time and went to the trouble to do whatever to help them. He cultivated that friendship. He saw it as a worthwhile activity.

I was amused at a cartoon that appeared in a magazine. It was the picture of a thief wearing one of those "Lone Ranger" masks. His gun was pointed toward his frightened victim as he yelled: "Okay, gimmee all your valuables!"

The victim began stuffing into the sack all his *friends.*

How valuable are relationships to you? If you have trouble answering that, I'll help you decide. Stop and think back over the past month or two. How much of your leisure have you spent developing and enjoying relationships?

Jesus, God's Son, certainly considered the relationship He had with His disciples worth His time. They spent literally hours together. They ate together and wept together, and I'm sure they must have laughed together as well. Being God, He really didn't "need" those men. He certainly didn't need the hassle they created on occasion. But He loved those twelve men. He believed in them. They had a special relationship, a lot like Paul, Silas, and Timothy;

David and Jonathan; Barnabas and John Mark; and Elijah and Elisha.

As the poet Samuel Taylor Coleridge once put it, "Friendship is a sheltering tree."[3] How very true! Whatever leisure time we are able to invest in relationships is time well spent. And when we do, let's keep in mind we are "imitating God," for His Son certainly did.

HOW TO IMPLEMENT LEISURE

The bottom line of all this, of course, is actually *doing* it. We can nod in agreement until we turn blue, but our greatest need is not inclination; it's demonstration.

Here are two suggestions that will help.

1. *Deliberately stop being absorbed with the endless details of life.* Our Savior said it straight when He declared that we cannot, at the same time, serve both God and man. But we try so hard! If Jesus' words from Matthew 6 are saying anything, they are saying, "Don't sweat the things only God can handle." Each morning, deliberately decide not to allow worry to steal your time and block your leisure.

2. *Consciously start taking time for leisure.* After God put the world together, He rested. We are commanded to imitate Him.

For the rest to occur in our lives, Christ Jesus must be in proper focus. He must be in His rightful place before we can ever expect to get our world to fall into place.

A bone-weary father dragged into his home dog-tired late one evening. It had been one of those unbelievable days of pressure, deadlines, and demands. He looked forward to a time of relaxation and quietness. Exhausted, he picked up the evening paper and headed for his favorite easy chair by the fireplace. About the time he got his shoes untied, plop! Into his lap dropped his five-year-old son with a big grin.

"Hi, Dad . . . let's play!"

He loved his boy dearly, but his need for a little time all alone to repair and think was, for the moment, a greater need than time with Junior. But how could he maneuver it?

There had been a recent moon probe, and the newspaper

carried a huge picture of earth. With a flash of much-needed insight, the dad asked his boy to bring a pair of scissors and some transparent tape. Quickly, he cut the picture of earth into various shapes and sizes, then handed the homemade jigsaw puzzle over to his son in a pile.

"You tape it all back together, Danny, then come on back and we'll play, okay?"

Off scampered the child to his room as Dad breathed a sigh of relief. But in less than ten minutes the boy bounded back with everything taped in perfect place. Stunned, the father asked, "How'd you do it so fast, son?"

"Aw, it was easy, Daddy. You see, there's this picture of a man on the back of the sheet . . . and when you put the man together, the world comes together."

So it is in life. When we put the Man in His rightful place, it's amazing what happens to our world. And, more importantly, what happens to us. I can assure you that in the final analysis of your life—when you stop some day and look back on the way you spent your time—your use of leisure will be far more important than those hours you spent with your nose to the grindstone. Don't wait until it's too late to enjoy life.

Live it up now. Throw yourself into it with abandonment. Get up out of the rut of work long enough to see that there's more to life than a job and a paycheck. You'll never be the same! Your stress fractures will heal.

To put it another way, when you forget all those mice in London, you'll start having the time of your life.

———◦———

Lord, our God,

Habits and fears, guilt and discontentment have teamed up against us and pinned us to the mat of monotony.

We find ourselves running in a tight radius, like a rat in a sewer pipe. Our world has become too small, too routine, too grim. Although busy, we have to confess that a nagging sense of boredom has now boarded our ship in this journey of life. We are enduring the scenery instead of enjoying it. We really take ourselves too seriously . . . and our stress continues to multiply.

We desire change . . . a cure from this terminal illness of dullness and routine.

We are sheep, not rats. You have made us whole people who are free to think and relax in leisure, not slaves chained to a schedule. Enable us to break loose! Show us ways to do that. Give us the courage to start today and the hope we need to stay fresh tomorrow . . . and the next day, and the next.

Bring the child out from within us. Introduce us again to the sounds and smells and sights of this beautiful world you wrapped around us. Convince us of the importance of friendships and laughter and wonder. Put our world back together.

May we become people like Your Son, committed to the highest standard of excellence and devotion to Your will, yet easy to live with and at peace within.

In His strong name we pray,
Amen.

CHAPTER NINE

DESTINY

Most of us don't like to contemplate subjects like death—or life after death—until circumstances grab us by the collar and force us to stare the questions in the face.

We lose a close friend, a spouse, a parent, a child . . . and suddenly life-and-death issues no longer seem vague and foggy. Suddenly, they are very real and must somehow be dealt with.

Even more shocking is when the death we contemplate is our own. The doctor calls us back into his or her office and presents us with facts we don't want to hear and don't know how to handle. A life that seemed somehow interminable—indestructible—is reduced to a matter of months . . . perhaps weeks.

Suddenly, issues like "eternal destiny" snap into sharp focus. Suddenly questions about our soul and salvation seem incredibly relevant. Questions we once hesitated to ponder or voice now cry out to be answered . . .

"How can I know God in a meaningful way?"

"What must I do to guarantee eternal life with my Maker?"

"Is there some way I can be certain that I will go to heaven?"

"Will you explain in simple, nontechnical terms what it means to be born again?"

"I'm guilty because I haven't lived a clean life. How can the Lord forgive me?"

"I've been a fairly religious person, but I lack a deep and abiding peace with God . . . why?"

"What does the Bible say about life after death?"
"Did Jesus actually die for me?"
"What, exactly, is the gospel?"
    Whether or not these questions are verbalized, they are the ones most people think about, especially when death seems near. They are good questions that deserve an answer. They are also searching questions that have to do with an issue of utmost importance—receiving eternal life from God. Forgiveness forever. This is not something that calls for a lot of opinions. Theological double-talk will do nothing to mend the deep stress fractures we feel. The insights must come from the Bible, and they need to be so clear that anybody can understand them. They also have to make sense.
    Here is a scriptural, simple, sensible answer for those who wonder about the single most significant subject in all of life: salvation.

B eing lost is a terrifying experience. A person's head spins as panic creeps up, shouting threats like, "You'll never find your way!" or "It's impossible!" Fear clutches at you.
    When I was about eight years old, I remember being lost downtown in the busy metropolis of Houston, Texas. My mother had told me to stay in the toy department of a store while she went down the street to pick up a package she was having gift-wrapped. I continued to play for a few minutes, but soon lost interest. So I decided to leave the store and walk down to where my mom had gone. Poor decision. I turned the wrong way, so I was going in the opposite direction, all the time being absolutely sure it was the right way.
    I must have walked four long blocks before I realized my mistake. I thought, "Maybe it's across the street." My heart began beating faster as I trotted over to the other side, but I still couldn't find the store. By then I had run four, five, six blocks . . . still no sign of that familiar storefront.
    By then I was crying. I didn't know who to ask for help . . . everybody seemed so unconcerned. My mind was seized with such fear that I couldn't even remember the name of the store where

she said she was going or even the store I had left twenty minutes before. I circled back toward the direction I began—or so I thought—but in my bewildered state, I had made yet another miscalculation, for nothing looked at all familiar now.

To this day, I distinctly recall the awful sense of desperation and confusion. Guilt assaulted me as I said to myself again and again, *Why didn't I do as Mama told me? Why didn't I obey?*

The strange part of it all was that there were people all around me—hundreds of them—and within a few feet there were cars moving in both directions. There was also a policeman at each intersection, as well as numerous employees and merchants inside every store I passed. There I was, darting here and there amongst all that humanity, but I could not have felt *more* lost in the thick jungles along the Amazon!

Through the kindness of a total stranger who saw my plight and took the time to escort me back to the original toy department, I was rescued and reunited with my concerned, loving mother. Although I am more than fifty years removed from that horrible episode, I vividly remember how terrifying it was . . . to be lost.

Several strange things are true about being lost. One is that we can think we really aren't when we are. Sincerity is no guarantee we're on the right road. Furthermore, we don't have to be alone to be lost. We can be surrounded by a lot of folks—even a large group of nice people—and be totally off track. Running faster doesn't help, either. Speed, like sincerity, is no friend to the bewildered.

One more thought: We can't trust our feelings or our hunches to solve our dilemma. We need help from something or someone outside ourselves. A map. A person who knows the way. Whatever or whoever . . . we must have accurate assistance.

HURTLING TOWARD A DESTINY . . . UNAWARE

It's interesting to note that one of the terms the Bible uses to describe people who don't know God in a personal and meaningful manner is "lost." That doesn't necessarily mean they are immoral or lawless or bad neighbors or financial failures or emotionally unstable or irresponsible or even unfriendly folks. Just lost.

As we've already observed, they may be sincere, involved, in touch with many people, and moving rapidly (and successfully) through life. They may even feel good about themselves—confident, secure, enthusiastic . . . yet still lost. Physically active and healthy, yet spiritually off track. Sincerely deluded. Unconsciously moving through life and out of touch with the One who made them. Disconnected from the living God.

Take a close look at this statement I've copied from the old, reliable book of Proverbs in the Bible.

> *There is a way which seems right to a man, but its end is the way of death (Proverbs 14:12).*

Isn't that penetrating? The "way" a person is going through life may seem right. It may have the appearance of being okay. It may also have the approval and admiration of other rather influential individuals. But its end result is the ultimate dead-end street.

All this reminds me of a true yet tragic World War II story. The *Lady-Be-Good* was a bomber whose crew was a well-seasoned flight team, a group of intelligent and combat-ready airmen. After a successful bombing mission, they were returning to home base late one night. In front of the pilot and copilot was a panel of instruments and radar equipment they had to rely on to reach their final destination. They had made the flight many times before, so they knew about how long it took to return.

But this flight was different. Unaware of a strong tailwind that pushed the bomber much more rapidly through the night air than usual, the men in the cockpit looked in amazement at their instruments as they correctly signaled it was time to land.

The crew, however, refused to believe those accurate dials and gauges. Confident that they were still miles away from home, they kept flying and hoping, looking intently for those familiar lights below. The fuel supply was finally depleted. The big olive drab bomber never made it back. It was found deep in the desert many miles further and many days later. Its fine crew had all perished, having overshot the field by a great distance . . . because they followed the promptings of their own feelings, which "seemed right" but proved wrong. Dead wrong.

What happened in the air back in the early 1940s is happening in principle every day on earth. There are good, sincere, well-meaning, intelligent people traveling on a collision course with death, yet totally unaware of their destiny. That's why we read that Jesus, God's great Son, came ". . . to seek and to save that which was lost" (Luke 19:10). His coming to earth was God's seek-and-save mission designed to help those who are lost find the right way home.

That needs some explanation.

Think of the Bible as the absolutely reliable instrument panel designed to get people (and to keep people) on the right track. We won't be confused if we believe its signals and respond to its directions, even though we may not "feel" in agreement at times. In this Book we find a bold yet true statement:

> . . . *God has given us eternal life, and this life is in His Son. He who has the Son has the life; he who does not have the Son of God does not have the life.*
>
> *These things I have written to you who believe in the name of the Son of God, in order that you may know that you have eternal life (1 John 5:11b–13).*

Read that again, this time a little more slowly and, if possible, aloud.

SALVATION OFFERED—FREE

It doesn't take a Ph.D. in English Literature to observe that God is offering a gift. The gift is eternal life, which is directly connected to His Son. Now let's be clear and cautious. Becoming a member of a church is not mentioned here—just believing in the Son of God, Jesus Christ. Neither does God require a long list of heavy-duty accomplishments. Nor vast sums of money. God is coming to the rescue of those who are lost by offering the free gift of eternal life to those who will simply believe. Those who do may know they have been rescued.

No mumbo-jumbo, no tricks, no divinely hidden agenda, no cleverly concealed conditions. The lost can know they are on the right road by trusting what God is signaling from His panel of truth. Believe Him!

"But it seems too easy," you say. "Something as vital as eternal salvation seems far more valuable than that." Don't misunderstand. It *is* valuable . . . the most priceless possession one can have. But because we don't have to work for it or pay for it does not mean it's cheap or that nobody paid a handsome price. Someone did. His name? Jesus. Perhaps you already forgot that this gift of salvation is directly connected to God's Son, Christ Himself. Because He paid the full price, because He opened the way for us, we are able to take it as a gift.

It's funny, but most of us are suspicious of free gifts. "There ain't no such thing as a free lunch" is more than a line out of a comedian's script. We have too much skepticism (or pride) to believe we can get something for nothing. Any time we are approached by an individual who promises, "Here, take it; it's yours, *free*," we are wary. We usually don't reach out and accept it. So it's understandable that we'd be reluctant to accept a gift as important as eternal salvation if it has the appearance of a "free lunch," right?

THE COST OF ETERNAL SALVATION

In all honesty, to say that God's rescue offer costs nobody anything is misleading. It costs *us* nothing today, but it cost His Son's life. That's the part we forget about.

When sin first reared its ugly head on earth, the holy God of heaven could no longer enjoy a close relationship with the human race. And the longer mankind practiced his or her wicked ways, the wider the gap grew between man and God. This sin disease, contracted at birth and inescapably contagious, spread like wildfire from one generation to the next. With sin came death, as this verse of Scripture declares:

> *When Adam sinned, sin entered the entire human race.*
> *His sin spread death throughout all the world, so everything*
> *began to grow old and die, for all sinned (Romans 5:12, TLB).*

Yes, everything. In fact, this universal sin disease impacted every part of our being. Hard as it may be to read these words, please do so:

> As the Scriptures say, "No one is good—no one in all the world is innocent." No one has ever really followed God's paths, or even truly wanted to. Every one has turned away; all have gone wrong. No one anywhere has kept on doing what is right; not one. Their talk is foul and filthy like the stench from an open grave. Their tongues are loaded with lies. Everything they say has in it the sting and poison of deadly snakes. Their mouths are full of cursing and bitterness. They are quick to kill, hating anyone who disagrees with them. Wherever they go they leave misery and trouble behind them, and they have never known what it is to feel secure or enjoy God's blessing. They care nothing about God nor what he thinks of them (Romans 3:10–18, TLB).

Talk about descriptive! But that's the way we are in God's sight. Being lost, we are in such a miserable spiritual condition that we have no hope of finding our way to Him on our own. Sin separates us from our Creator. His rightful requirement is that sin must be punished. Someone who is qualified must rescue mankind by satisfying God's wrath against sin. Someone must pay the awful price, dying as our substitute, taking our place and bearing our sin before God.

Jesus Christ did just that.

Don't simply believe my words . . . believe the words from the Bible:

> For God took the sinless Christ and poured into him our sins. Then, in exchange, he poured God's goodness into us! (2 Corinthians 5:21, TLB).

> We aren't saved from sin's grasp by knowing the commandments of God, because we can't and don't keep them, but God put into effect a different plan to save us. He sent his own Son in a human body like ours—except that ours are sinful—

*and destroyed sin's control over us by giving himself as a sacri-
fice for our sins (Romans 8:3, TLB).*

*For God loved the world so much that he gave his only
Son so that anyone who believes in him shall not perish but
have eternal life. . . . And all who trust him—God's Son—to
save them have eternal life; those who don't believe and obey
him shall never see heaven, but the wrath of God remains upon
them (John 3:16, 36, TLB).*

*Christ also suffered. He died once for the sins of all us
guilty sinners, although he himself was innocent of any sin at
any time, that he might bring us safely home to God (1 Peter
3:18, TLB).*

*Under this new plan we have been forgiven and made
clean by Christ's dying for us once and for all. Under the old
agreement the priests stood before the altar day after day offering sacrifices that could never take away our sins. But Christ
gave himself to God for our sins as one sacrifice for all time, and
then sat down in the place of highest honor at God's right hand
(Hebrews 10:10–12, TLB).*

THE ONLY UNRESOLVED ISSUE ABOUT SALVATION

Yes, it certainly cost somebody something. I repeat, it cost
Jesus Christ His life. But because He paid the price in full on our
behalf, we are able to accept God's offer free and clear of any cost
to us. The payment has been made. The ransom has been provided
in full.

The only issue that remains is this: Will you accept the gift
God offers you today? Now that the remedy for sin has been provided, all that remains is receiving it . . . not having every related
question answered.

Picture a person helplessly trapped on the sixth floor of a
burning hotel. The elevators no longer function, the stairways are
flaming infernos. To live, the person must leap into a net which
firemen down below are holding ready. Imagine the trapped man
screaming from his broken window, "I will not jump until you give

me a satisfactory explanation of several things: (1) How did this fire get started? (2) Why has it spread so quickly? (3) What happened to the sprinkler system? and (4) How do I know for sure that net will hold me? Until you guys can come up with some pretty substantial answers, I'm staying right here in Room 612!"

In like manner, the question as to why God allowed sin to enter the world or the need for airtight convincing proof is comparatively unimportant, even irrelevant, as we find ourselves lost, moving rapidly toward the grave, and destined for eternal condemnation. Slice it up and analyze it any way you wish, when we reduce our response to God's offer of salvation, it comes down to *faith*: being willing to abandon oneself, without reservation, to the eternal net God has spread . . . leaping while believing with absolute confidence that He will do as He promised. Remember, the other options are reduced to zero, according to God's plan.

WHAT ABOUT LIFE AFTER DEATH?

A chapter on this vital subject would be incomplete if nothing were said about life beyond the grave. Thanks to such authorities as Dr. Elizabeth Kubler-Ross and Raymond A. Moody, Jr., the issue of life after death is now being discussed openly. Numerous books—Christian and non-Christian—are now available, ranging from the bizarre to the skeptical. For the sake of space and dependability, let's limit our thoughts to the biblical record.

Jesus spoke openly about both heaven and hell. So did several others in Scripture. It is clear to all who read the Bible that everyone has an eternal soul . . . *everyone* has eternal life. The real question is, where will we spend that eternal life? Read the following verses carefully:

> And inasmuch as it is appointed for men to die once and after this comes judgment (Hebrews 9:27).

> And I say to you, that every careless word that men shall speak, they shall render account for it in the day of judgment (Matthew 12:36).

And these will go away into eternal punishment, but the righteous into eternal life (Matthew 25:46).

But you, why do you judge your brother? Or you again, why do you regard your brother with contempt? For we shall all stand before the judgment seat of God (Romans 14:10).

Jesus said to her, "I am the resurrection and the life; he who believes in Me shall live even if he dies, and everyone who lives and believes in Me shall never die. Do you believe this?" (John 11:25–26).

THE REALITY OF HELL

A particular story Jesus once told comes to my mind every time I think of life after death. Because it is descriptive and brief, we are able to get a fairly uncomplicated picture in our minds of this subject.

Now there was a certain rich man, and he habitually dressed in purple and fine linen, gaily living in splendor every day. And a certain poor man named Lazarus was laid at his gate, covered with sores, and longing to be fed with the crumbs which were falling from the rich man's table; besides, even the dogs were coming and licking his sores. Now it came about that the poor man died and he was carried away by the angels to Abraham's bosom; and the rich man also died and was buried. And in Hades he lifted up his eyes, being in torment, and saw Abraham far away, and Lazarus in his bosom. And he cried out and said, "Father Abraham, have mercy on me, and send Lazarus, that he may dip the tip of his finger in water and cool off my tongue; for I am in agony in this flame."

But Abraham said, "Child, remember that during your life you received your good things, and likewise Lazarus bad things; but now he is being comforted here, and you are in agony. And besides all this, between us and you there is a great chasm fixed, in order that those who wish to come over from here to you may not be able, and that none may cross over from there to us."

And he said, "Then I beg you, Father, that you send him to my father's house—for I have five brothers—that he may warn them, lest they also come to this place of torment."

But Abraham said, "They have Moses and the Prophets; let them hear them."

But he said, "No, Father Abraham, but if someone goes to them from the dead, they will repent!"

But he said to him, "If they do not listen to Moses and the Prophets, neither will they be persuaded if someone rises from the dead" (Luke 16:19–31).

Much of what you just read needs no explanation. It is the story of two men. While alive, their status could hardly have been more different. And when they died, again a contrast. One found himself in heaven; the other, in hell. Our attention falls upon the rich man who is pleading for relief and removal from his torturous surroundings. The scene is unpleasant to imagine, but it is nevertheless real. Neither here nor elsewhere does Jesus suggest this was merely a fantasy.

The man in hell is in conscious torment. He is crying out for mercy. Being "far away" (v. 23) and permanently removed by "a great chasm" (v. 26), he is desperately alone, unable to escape from hell, as we read, "none may cross over" (v. 26). The horror is painfully literal, unlike the jokes often passed around regarding hell. Haunted with thoughts of other family members ultimately coming to the same place, the man begs for someone to go to his father's house and warn his brothers ". . . lest they also come to this place of torment" (v. 28).

This is only one of many references to an eternal existence in hell. The New Testament, in fact, says more about hell than it does about heaven. Here are just a few characteristics of hell set forth in the New Testament.

- It is a place of weeping and gnashing of teeth (Matthew 8:12).
- It is a place where people scream for mercy, have memories, are tormented, feel alone, cannot escape (Luke 16:23–31).

- It is a place of unquenchable fire (Mark 9:48).
- It is a place of darkness (Revelation 9:2).
- It is a place of eternal damnation (Mark 3:29, KJV).
- It is a place where God's wrath is poured out (Revelation 14:10, KJV).
- It is a place of everlasting destruction (2 Thessalonians 1:9).

The finality of all this is overwhelmingly depressing. We have little struggle believing that heaven will be forever, but for some reason, we ignore that hell will be equally everlasting. To deny the permanence of hell is impossible without also removing the permanence of heaven. Each is a reality, and each is ultimate finality.

Many views try to explain away or bypass hell. One attempt is *annihilation*. This says that the righteous will live eternally, but the wicked will ultimately be judged and destroyed. Nice idea but a theological cop-out. It cannot be maintained by a serious and intelligent study of Scripture . . . for example, the whole issue of a bodily resurrection. What purpose is the resurrection if the lost are to be extinguished forever?

Another attempt at bypassing hell is *universalism*, which teaches that all humanity will ultimately be saved. This position offers a comforting "redemptive mercy" that will eventually include all mankind. If this were true, what did Jesus mean when He talked about the very real possibility of being lost forever? "Should not perish" in John 3:16 implies that some will indeed perish. And how could His comment be taken seriously when He says to the unsaved, "Depart from Me, accursed ones, into the eternal fire" (Matthew 25:41)? Count on it, friend, eternal means eternal.

THE REALITY OF HEAVEN

The same Bible that develops the subject of hell also reveals the truth about heaven. What is heaven like? Playing harps all day? Lounging around on Cloud Nine? Living in enormous mansions along solid gold streets? Does it mean we'll all have long white robes with matching sandals, glowing halos, and big flapping wings? Hardly!

Heaven is an actual place. A prepared place, designed for God's redeemed people, those who have accepted God's free gift of His Son.

> *Let not your heart be troubled; believe in God, believe also in Me. In My Father's house are many dwelling places; if it were not so, I would have told you; for I go to prepare a place for you. And if I go and prepare a place for you, I will come again, and receive you to Myself; that where I am, there you may be also" (John 14:1–3).*

According to this and other New Testament verses, heaven will be a place of beauty, peace, constant health, and happiness, filled with people from all the earthly ages who have one thing in common: faith in the Lord Jesus Christ, the Lamb of God, who took away the sin of the world.

Think of it! Characters from the Old Testament like Moses, David, Rahab, Elijah, Abraham, Joseph, Esther, Job, Daniel, and the other godly prophets will converse with John, Peter, Matthew, James, Paul, Silas, Barnabas, Mary, Elizabeth, Lydia, and Andrew. We'll be able to enjoy close conversations with church history's great Christians, like Augustine, Livingstone, Hudson Taylor, Martin Luther, Calvin, Knox, Spurgeon, Moody, Wycliffe, and Huss (to name only a few), plus those unknown martyrs, missionaries, pastors, authors, statesmen, politicians, poets, and leaders from every generation since time began. Stupendous thought!

More amazing still, in heaven we'll have a face-to-face, exclusive relationship with our Savior, gloriously enjoyed without interruption or heartache or grief or sin or the threat of death.

> *And I saw a new heaven and a new earth; for the first heaven and the first earth passed away, and there is no longer any sea. And I saw the holy city, new Jerusalem, coming down out of heaven from God, made ready as a bride adorned for her husband. And I heard a loud voice from the throne, saying, "Behold, the tabernacle of God is among men, and He shall dwell among them, and they shall be His people, and God Himself shall be among them, and He shall wipe away every*

tear from their eyes; and there shall no longer be any death;
there shall no longer be any mourning, or crying, or pain; the
first things have passed away. And He who sits on the throne
said, "Behold, I am making all things new." And He said,
"Write, for these words are faithful and true." And He said to
me, "It is done. I am the Alpha and the Omega, the beginning
and the end. I will give to the one who thirsts from the spring
of the water of life without cost (Revelation 21:1–6).

There it is again. "Without cost." Heaven will be the destiny of those who take God at His Word, believing in His Son, Jesus Christ, and coming, by faith, to salvation . . . without cost.

Can something this good really be free? Even free of works? You decide after reading these Scripture verses.

For by grace you have been saved through faith; and
that not of yourselves, it is the gift of God; not as a result of
works, that no one should boast (Ephesians 2:8–9).

Being justified as a gift by His grace through the
redemption which is in Christ Jesus (Romans 3:24).

Now to the one who works, his wage is not reckoned as
a favor, but as what is due. But to the one who does not work,
but believes in Him who justifies the ungodly, his faith is reck-
oned as righteousness (Romans 4:4–5).

He saved us, not on the basis of deeds which we have
done in righteousness, but according to His mercy, by the wash-
ing of regeneration and renewing by the Holy Spirit, whom
He poured out upon us richly through Jesus Christ our Savior,
that being justified by His grace we might be made heirs
according to the hope of eternal life (Titus 3:5–7).

Knowing that you were not redeemed with perishable
things like silver or gold from your futile way of life inherited
from your forefathers, but with precious blood, as of a lamb
unblemished and spotless, the blood of Christ (1 Peter
1:18–19).

Nevertheless knowing that a man is not justified by the works of the Law but through faith in Christ Jesus, even we have believed in Christ Jesus, that we may be justified by faith in Christ, and not by the works of the Law; since by the works of the Law shall no flesh be justified (Galatians 2:16).

Who has saved us, and called us with a holy calling, not according to our works, but according to His own purpose and grace which was granted us in Christ Jesus from all eternity, but now has been revealed by the appearing of our Savior Christ Jesus, who abolished death, and brought life and immortality to light through the gospel (2 Timothy 1:9–10).

Yes, salvation comes to us "free and clear" of any hidden charges or religious deeds or human effort. We come to God through Christ . . . lost, sinful, without hope, and deserving of hell. In grace, He sees us in Christ and in grace loves us, forgives us, accepts us into His family, and promises us an eternal home with Him in heaven, the ultimate destination of all His people.

YOUR FINAL DESTINATION: WHERE?

Salvation is the single most important issue in all of life. Yet, if we are not careful, we'll put it off until later; we'll even put it completely out of our minds. This chapter has helped us to realize salvation is an urgent matter. We dare not postpone our decision!

In review:

- We are lost.
- We are sinful.
- We need help.
- God is holy.
- Christ has died.
- Salvation is free.
- Hell is horrible.
- Heaven is available.
- We must believe.

For I delivered to you as of first importance what I also received, that Christ died for our sins according to the Scriptures, and that He was buried, and that He was raised on the third day according to the Scriptures (1 Corinthians 15:3–4).

. . . God has given us eternal life, and this life is in His Son. He who has the Son has the life; he who does not have the Son of God does not have the life. These things I have written to you who believe in the name of the Son of God, in order that you may know that you have eternal life (1 John 5:11b–13).

- You can know.
- Will you believe?

I read these words recently:

> The reality of life beyond the grave should make every one of us ponder our eternal destination, because the Bible teaches only two possibilities, heaven and hell.
>
> We take care to provide for the relatively short span of retirement after 65. How foolish not to plan for the endless ages of eternity. Confrontation with what comes after death caused one young man to prepare for the hereafter by receiving Jesus Christ as his Savior. He was looking at a large estate one day and said to a friend, "Oh, if I were lucky enough to call this estate mine, I should be a happy fellow. It's worth a quarter million."
>
> "And then?" said his friend.
>
> "Why, then I'd pull down the old house and build a mansion, have lots of friends around me, get married, have several fine cars and keep the finest horses and dogs in the country."
>
> "And then?"
>
> "Then I would hunt, and ride, and fish, and keep open house, and enjoy life gloriously."
>
> "And then?"
>
> "Why, then, I suppose like other people, I should grow old and not care so much for these things."
>
> "And then?"
>
> "Why, in the course of nature I should die."
>
> "And then?"

"Oh, brother . . . you and your 'and then.' I have no time for you now!"

Years later the friend was surprised to hear from him, "God bless you. I owe my happiness to you."

"How?"

"By two words asked at the right time— 'And then?'"[1]

Salvation is yours for the taking. I ask you, will you do so today?

———◈———

Loving God, thank You for accepting me and forgiving me many years ago when I was lost, and afraid, and confused, and so far away from You. I am thankful that You heard my prayer and took me seriously, even though I did not know how to express my faith in Jesus very well. All I knew to do was to come as a little child, which I did. And You graciously took me in. Thank You for making it possible to KNOW eternal life with You—today.

Now I come to You on behalf of this person who is reading these words right now. Please help that individual come to terms with what he or she has read. Take away the fear and the doubt. Push aside the tendency to procrastinate. Reveal the urgency of this decision. May Your Son's death and resurrection be convincing so that this person may KNOW eternal life with You—today.

With confidence, I ask this in the strong name of Jesus Christ, my Lord and Savior,

Amen.

CHAPTER TEN

DEMONISM

There are some stresses that go beyond the realm of the "natural." There are some pressures that cannot be explained in mere emotional or psychological terms. I'm speaking of intense spiritual pressures that can assault both non-Christians and Christians alike. People in the world may try to laugh it off, and people on the liberal fringes of Christendom may scoff or seek to explain it away . . . but demonism is neither funny nor phony.

It is real. It is, in fact, as serious and significant a subject as can ever be considered. But, strangely, it remains one of those unmentionables. Almost like, "Let's not talk about it, and maybe it will go away." We Christians avoid it like the plague. And when we do discuss it, our comments fall somewhere between traditional superstition and downright ignorance.

Even though we have ignored it, the world has exploited it. By twisting the truth and pushing the hot buttons of human curiosity and gross sensuality, slick promoters have turned it into a money-making extravaganza . . . a weird sideshow attraction with all the crowd-pleasing gimmicks. And the devil (yes, friend, there IS a personal devil) could not be happier. The last thing he wants is to have his presence and his strategy exposed.

Although brief, this chapter is an attempt to draw back the thick veil of fear and uncertainty about our adversary. Christians need to be informed of the truth: that we have the victory; that we are more than conquerors rather than helpless victims when it comes to dealing with

Satan and his demons. If you are interested in what God has promised, what protection you possess, and what techniques you can use with confidence, this chapter is for you.

———•———

The church of Jesus Christ lost a gallant warrior of the faith with the passing of Merrill F. Unger. It was my choice privilege to study Hebrew under this fine Semitic scholar during my years in seminary. He may be gone in body, but certainly not in memory. Anyone who sat under Dr. Unger's teaching will never forget his devotion to the Lord Jesus Christ, which was revealed in his unique prayers before every class session, and his dedication to the truth of Scripture.

Of special interest to Dr. Unger throughout his ministry was the subject of demonism. Although he has gone home to be with the Lord he loved so dearly, his zeal and insights have been preserved in several books on that subject which he left in his legacy. One I would heartily recommend is entitled *Demons in the World Today*. In that volume these words appear:

> Certainly there is no excuse for the church to surrender its charismatic power to heal and deliver from satanic oppression. In the very measure that it does, it advertises its spiritual bankruptcy and makes itself a weak institution that no longer commands the respect of the spiritually needy masses. No wonder multitudes are seeking spiritual reality in Oriental religions, non-Christian faiths, and occult-oriented perversions of Christianity. Christian faith is so devitalized by apostasy and so contaminated with men's opinions and a defective presentation of Jesus Christ that it is becoming a hollow shell, powerless to affect men's lives.[1]

I couldn't agree more completely. Long enough have Christians taken a tongue-in-cheek approach to the issue of demonism! It is time for us to stand up, stand firm, and stand against the powers of darkness in the strength of our Lord Jesus

Christ. Boldly and confidently, we have every right to deny the adversary any ground he attempts to claim by means of trickery and intimidation.

IGNORANCE MUST BE DISPELLED

There appears in 2 Corinthians 2:11 a short but powerful statement concerning the devil: "in order that no advantage be taken of us by Satan; for we are not ignorant of his schemes."

The writer's concern is that the Corinthian believers fully and completely forgive an individual in their local church. They are told to reaffirm their love for him (v. 8) and to prove their obedience (v. 9) by not restraining themselves in this act of forgiveness.

Why? So Satan would not be able to take advantage of that situation. In other words, their sustained lack of forgiveness would give the enemy an opportunity to wedge his way into their fellowship and accomplish his insidious objectives. Their disobedience could become the adversary's ground of entrance. He patiently awaits such open doors and cleverly makes his moves at such times.

But what does Paul declare? He says, "We are not ignorant of his schemes." In effect, he is saying, "We know his style. We are constantly aware of his methods and strategy. He doesn't have us fooled!"

Strong, confident, reassuring words. But are they true of *you?* Paul could say that, but can *you?*

Before any opponent can be intelligently withstood, one must have a knowledge of his ways. Ignorance must be dispelled. No boxer in his right mind enters the ring without having first studied his opponent's style. The same is true on the football field. Or the battlefield. Days (sometimes months) are spent studying the tactics, the weaknesses, the strengths of the opponent. Ignorance is an enemy to victory.

I urge you to make a serious study—on your own, from the Bible—of the devil and his host of demons. This chapter cannot do that for you, but it can be a source of motivation. Remember, ignorance of the enemy puts you at his mercy and steals the confidence from you that you need to stand against his strategy. *Inform yourself!*

ARMOR MUST BE WORN

Turn next in your Bible to Ephesians 6:10–14. These five verses will prove to be very helpful in your understanding of the ongoing battle. I would suggest you memorize them during the next several days.

> *Finally, be strong in the Lord, and in the strength of His might. Put on the full armor of God, that you may be able to stand firm against the schemes of the devil. For our struggle is not against flesh and blood, but against the rulers, against the powers, against the world forces of this darkness, against the spiritual forces of wickedness in the heavenly places. Therefore, take up the full armor of God, that you may be able to resist in the evil day, and having done everything, to stand firm. Stand firm therefore . . .*

A close look will reveal four two-word commands. Get a pencil and underscore each one.

Verse 10: Be strong!
Verse 11: Put on!
Verse 13: Take up!
Verse 14: Stand firm!

Let's spend a few minutes thinking about each one before we move on to the actual strategies we can employ against demonic attacks.

Be Strong!

Because the battle is an invisible warfare, our strength is not external. This refers to inner strength, as the tenth verse concludes, ". . . in the strength of His might," referring to the Lord Jesus Christ. We are to be strong in Him. Lean on Him, by faith. Turn to Him in prayer. Walk with Him in confident trust, drawing upon *His* power.

Why? This is best answered in another section of the New Testament.

> *And when you were dead in your transgressions and the uncircumcision of your flesh, He made you alive together with*

*Him, having forgiven us all our transgressions, having can-
celed out the certificate of debt consisting of decrees against us
and which was hostile to us; and He has taken it out of the way,
having nailed it to the cross. When He had disarmed the rulers
and authorities, He made a public display of them, having triumphed over them through Him (Colossians 2:13–15).*

At the cross, when Christ Jesus died, He "disarmed" all creatures of darkness. He "triumphed over them." So then, He is the
champion. When you turn to Him for strength, you are turning to
the One who has sovereign authority over them. He won it at the
cross. Be strong in the strength of the Champion.

Put On!

Put on what? Ephesians 6:11 spells it out. We are to wear
"the full armor of God" so we may be able to stand firm against the
enemy's schemes. Good troops who fight well are well equipped.
Inferior weapons and poor equipment spell sure defeat.

Each piece of the armor is explained in Ephesians 6:14–17
(read verses 14 through 17 slowly and carefully), and each is
extremely important. The armor is designed to protect you and
give you confidence in combat. Now I warn you, when you realize
that this fight is unlike any other, it is easy to become fearful, intimidated, and shy. When you realize you cannot actually see the
enemy but he can see you, you are naturally seized with panic.

All the more reason to put on the armor God has provided.
Put it on, Christian.

Take Up!

It is there, available and waiting to be claimed. The full supply is yours, tailor-made to fit your personality, your set of circumstances, and your need. Reach out by faith and mentally "take
up" the armor of God. You'll learn how to use it in days to come;
but first, grab hold of it.

The day after I joined the Marine Corps, I found myself in
a room full of green, raw, frightened recruits. We were issued a sea
bag full of clothing plus a rifle, a cartridge belt, a bayonet, and a
heavy steel helmet. We were also provided with a "bucket issue" . . .

the basic supplies for our hygienic needs (the Corps had another name for it!). There we stood, scared and ignorant. Lowly privates not at all aware of what was ahead of us. Within the next thirteen weeks, we would discover how to wear and use everything, but for the time being, we were given one loud command: "Pick it up!" That's what God says to you today.

Stand Firm!

This is so important that the same words appear three separate times (Ephesians 6:11, 13, 14). These are the words of confidence and assurance. They tell us we have nothing to be afraid of. Nothing. After all, the One who does the fighting for us is the Champion. And the enemy is already defeated—it happened at the cross, remember? Of course, he doesn't want you to know that. Which explains why his favorite strategy is deception. He will throw up smoke screens that may appear terrifying and scary and awfully impressive . . . but behind all that noise and smoke is a full awareness that he is defeated.

So whatever you do in dealing with demons, Christian, do it with confidence. With absolute, victorious assurance. He is the victim; you are the victor. So stand firm!

RESISTING THE ENEMY

In the thirteenth verse of this same section of Scripture (Ephesians 6), we are told the purpose of our putting on the armor and standing firm.

. . . *that you may be able to resist in the evil day* . . .

Such days will come.

Some of you who read my words are very much aware of "the evil day." You have been harassed and attacked and badgered by the enemy. These attacks have come either against yourself or someone else . . . or both. Others of you are inexperienced and can only imagine what is involved in demonic oppression. Take it from me, it is horrible. It is ugly. It is vile. It is like nothing else you will ever encounter. It is exhausting and relentless. It is "evil," as the verse states. Satan may be a defeated foe, but he won't give up without a struggle.

Explanation of Demonic Involvement

We first need to understand the desire of our adversary. He wants, more than anything else, to have his way in the lives of humans. He wants to control us, or at least to win a hearing and become a persuasive force in our lives. His preferred realm of operation is our minds. This can be seen in the following two passages of Scripture:

> *For though we walk in the flesh, we do not war according to the flesh, for the weapons of our warfare are not of the flesh, but divinely powerful for the destruction of fortresses. We are destroying speculations and every lofty thing raised up against the knowledge of God, and we are taking every thought captive to the obedience of Christ (2 Corinthians 10:3–5).*

> *But I am afraid, lest as the serpent deceived Eve by his craftiness, your minds should be led astray from the simplicity and purity of devotion to Christ (2 Corinthians 11:3).*

Yes, that's it. "Led astray" says it best. It's the idea of getting us off course, sidetracked, pulled off target. Ultimately, his hope is to gain full control.

Because demons exist in spirit form (they have no physical bodies), they possess a strong desire to operate within a body, ideally a human body. All the more reason to "stand firm" against their strategy.

During our Lord's earthly ministry, He encountered demonized people on several occasions. (By the way, demon "possession" and demon "oppression" are not actual biblical terms. The Greek text supports only the idea of one being "demonized," which may include any one of several levels of demonic activity and/or control.) Sometimes the involvement was so deep that demons had to be expelled or exorcised from individuals. On other occasions, the person under attack was told to "resist." Resisting the enemy is mentioned in the Ephesians 6 passage we just looked at as well as James 4:7.

> *Submit therefore to God. Resist the devil and he will flee from you.*

This is a very practical instruction. No hocus-pocus. No repeating of the same word or phrase over and over again. No secret code or religious "mantra." Resisting means resisting. Shoving away. Pushing aside. Not allowing to stay or enter.

Suggestions for Resisting the Devil

Maybe a simple process to follow will help.

1. Vocally declare your faith in the Lord Jesus Christ. Use His full title as you do this. Openly acknowledge that He is your Master, your Lord, and the One who has conquered all other powers at the cross.

2. Deny any and all allegiance to the devil, his demonic host, and the occult. Do this forcefully and boldly. Again, express these things aloud.

3. Claim the full armor of God, based on Ephesians 6:10–17, as your complete protection. Read the passage orally with emphasis.

4. Finally, state firmly your resistance of demonic influence.

Consider using the following "Prayer of Resistance." Use it as a guide when you begin to feel afraid and sense the attack of evil forces.

> I do now renounce any and all allegiance I have ever given to Satan and his host of wicked spirits. I refuse to be influenced or intimidated by them. I refuse to be used by them in any way whatsoever. I reject all their attacks upon my body, my spirit, my soul, and my mind. I claim the shed blood of the Lord Jesus Christ throughout my being. And I revoke all their power and influence within me or round about me. I resist them in the name of my Lord and Master, Jesus Christ, the Champion over evil. I stand secure in the power of the cross of Calvary

whereby Satan and all his powers became defeated foes through the blood of my Lord Jesus Christ. I stand upon the promises of God's Word. In humble faith, I do here and now put on the whole armor of God that enables me to stand firm against the schemes of the devil.

While these words are certainly not "inspired," they may prove very helpful as you stand firm against the wicked one. I have found them helpful, personally.

One more thought about resisting: Claim the promise of James 4:7. Speaking of satanic opposition, James wrote:

> . . . *he will flee from you.*

Stand on that hope. Refuse the temptation to doubt the reality of God's promise to you. The enemy is defeated. He runs when you call his bluff. The blood of the cross carries with it divine clout. Fall back upon the transaction that occurred at the cross—Christ's blood for your sins.

CASTING OUT DEMONS

There are occasions when demons have become so entrenched within a life that the need to cast them out is evident. This is a much more emotional, wrenching experience and calls for help from other Christians. Scripture suggests resisting is something one does on his own, but when demons were actually expelled in biblical days, others were involved to assist in the process.

A Biblical Case Study

Several times in the Gospels and Acts we read of demons being exorcised. The example I'd like to refer to briefly is in Luke 8:26–33.

> *And they sailed to the country of the Gerasenes, which is opposite Galilee. And when He had come out onto the land, He was met by a certain man from the city who was possessed with demons; and who had not put on any clothing for a long time, and was not living in a house, but in the tombs. And seeing*

Jesus, he cried out and fell before Him, and said in a loud voice, "What do I have to do with You, Jesus, Son of the Most High God? I beg You, do not torment me." For He had been commanding the unclean spirit to come out of the man. For it had seized him many times; and he was bound with chains and shackles and kept under guard; and yet he would burst his fetters and be driven by the demon into the desert. And Jesus asked him, "What is your name?" And he said, "Legion"; for many demons had entered him. And they were entreating Him not to command them to depart into the abyss. Now there was a herd of many swine feeding there on the mountain; and the demons entreated Him to permit them to enter the swine. And He gave them permission. And the demons came out from the man and entered the swine; and the herd rushed down the steep bank into the lake, and were drowned.

The man Jesus met was demonized ("possessed" is not in the Greek text in verse 27). Within the man's person was the actual presence of evil forces—"many demons" (v. 30)—whose spokesman was named Legion. No need to repeat all the details of the man's demeanor, but obviously he bore the marks of torment. He had incredible strength and must have been a frightful sight.

Calmly and yet firmly, our Lord spoke to the demons within and, using the man's vocal cords, answers were given by Legion. Interestingly, the demons did not want to be sent to "the abyss," apparently a place of permanent removal, so Jesus allowed these demons to enter into a nearby herd of swine, which they did, and subsequently the pigs were drowned.

The man, now relieved of those tormenting spirits, is suddenly a changed individual. Look at the difference in verse 35:

And the people went out to see what had happened; and they came to Jesus, and found the man from whom the demons had gone out, sitting down at the feet of Jesus, clothed and in his right mind; and they became frightened.

Clothed and in his right mind, the man was wonderfully delivered by the power of the Son of God.

I mentioned earlier that the man had been "demonized." Perhaps it is advisable for me to amplify this a bit. Unless we understand what the presence of a demon (or demons) can do in a life, we'll lack the necessary compassion to assist those in desperate need.

An Explanation of Being "Demonized"

When one or more demons inhabit the body of an individual, that person finds himself under the control of the evil spirit(s). By temporarily blotting out his consciousness, the demon can speak and act through the victim, using him as his slave or tool. During such times (as we saw in Luke 8), the person often possesses incredible strength; a blasphemous, foul, vulgar tongue; a wild, violent temperament that goes to unbelievable extremes and frequently carries out dangerous actions against himself and others. It is not uncommon for the demonized victim to be driven to the most sadistic, brutal, and perverted forms of attack on others, to the ultimate extreme of murder.

It has been my observation that when a demon speaks and projects itself through its victim, the voice is different from the person's normal voice and personality. I have seen times when the evil spirit who speaks uses another language, totally unfamiliar to the victim. It is also interesting that the pronouns being used help you identify the presence of an alien being. The *first*-person pronoun ("I" and "me") consistently designates the inhabiting demon. Bystanders are addressed in the *second* person ("you" or "your"). The demonized victim is referred to in the *third* person ("him," "her," or "his") and is looked upon during the attack as unconscious and, for all practical purposes, nonexistent during this interval.

You will recall that the man in Luke 8 is virtually a passive "vehicle" used to carry about in his body the evil spirits. Naked, ferocious, and possessing superhuman strength, he was "driven by the demon" (v. 29). A very pathetic, descriptive scene. But after the demons were expelled, Dr. Luke informs us that the man was quiet, clothed, and completely under control (v. 35). The anguish and inner pressures were gone. In fact, if you read on in the Luke 8 account, you'll see that the man wanted to accompany the Lord

Jesus Christ. When told by the Savior not to do so but rather to go back home and announce what great things God had done for him, he gladly obeyed. There was a remarkable and sudden contrast that swept over the man once the demons were gone.

I have witnessed this on several occasions. Torment is replaced with a calm, quiet response; ugly and profane remarks are stopped and replaced with praise and gratitude to God. It is beautiful to behold!

A Necessary Warning to All

Bold confrontation is often needed. When people have become demonized, they need help—immediate, courageous, compassionate help. But let me warn you, spiritual warfare is no trifling matter! And lest you allow idle curiosity to draw you into the idea that such a ministry would be fun and games, *please proceed with caution.* No one becomes an "expert" in a deliverance ministry. Our only ground of victory over evil powers is our union with the Lord Jesus Christ. The spirits of darkness are unpredictable, extremely crafty, and ever so brilliant.

I draw upon the writing of Mark Bubeck for some "dos" and "don'ts" which will prove helpful. I've summarized what he has explained in greater detail in a book I heartily recommend, written by this capable author.

Here are the "don'ts":[2]

- *Don't* seek information or allow any wicked spirit to volunteer information you do not seek.
- *Don't* believe what a wicked spirit says unless you test it. They are inevitable liars like their leader, Satan.
- *Don't* be afraid of their threatening harm to you or your family.
- *Don't* assume that one victory is the end of the warfare.
- *Don't* rely upon bold confrontation as the main way to victory over the enemy. The positive application of doctrine, warfare praying, scripture memorization, and a walk of praise toward God are very essential.

And now some "dos":[3]

- *Do* daily put on the whole armor of God and claim your union with Christ and walk in the fullness of the Holy Spirit.
- *Do* take back all ground you may have given Satan by careless, willful sins of the flesh. A simple prayer of faith accomplishes this.
- *Do* bind all powers of darkness, commanding all of them to leave when the demon does.
- *Do* force the wicked spirit(s) to admit that because you are seated with Christ far above all principalities and powers (Ephesians 1:21, 2:6) that you have full authority over them.
- *Do* force them to admit that when you command them to leave, they have to go where Christ sends them.
- *Do* demand that if the wicked power has divided into several parts, that he become a whole spirit.
- *Do* be prepared for the wicked power to try to hurt the person you are working with in some manner. Sudden body pains, a severe headache, a choking experience, and the like are very often used.

Can a Christian Be Demonized?

For a number of years, I questioned this, but I am now convinced it can occur. If a "ground of entrance" has been granted the power of darkness (such as trafficking in the occult, a continual unforgiving spirit, a habitual state of carnality, etc.), the demon(s) sees this as a green light—okay to proceed (2 Corinthians 2:10–11, 1 Corinthians 5:1–5, Luke 22:31–32). Wicked forces are not discriminating with regard to which body they may inhabit. I have worked personally with troubled, anguished Christians for many years. On a few occasions, I have assisted in the painful process of relieving them of demons.

Perhaps a clarifying word of assurance is needed here. The believer *has* the Holy Spirit resident within. Therefore, the alien, wicked spirit certainly cannot claim "ownership" of the Christian. He is still a child of God. But while present within the body (perhaps in the region of the soul), that evil force can work havoc within a person's life, bringing the most extreme thoughts imaginable into his or her conscious awareness. Couldn't this explain how some believers can fall into and remain involved in such horrible sins? And how some could commit suicide?

Demon Confrontation Today

How does all this relate to us today? I have three factors in mind.

1. *There must be a correct diagnosis.* We need to guard against witch-hunting. Some people see demons in most every area of weakness or wrong. I've even heard of one man who believed a person he knew had "the demon of nail-biting." No, I doubt that biting one's fingernails is prompted by demons. Furthermore, there are characteristics among the mentally and emotionally disturbed that are bizarre, but not necessarily demonic. And there can be physical disorders as well. All of this tells us we must be very careful and discerning when it comes to diagnosis.

Some of the things to look for that might reveal demonism, however, are:

- sudden and unreasonable changes of moods;
- aggressive, unrestrainable expressions of hostility;
- unnatural attachment to charms, fortune-telling, and involvement in the occult;
- extreme, enslaving habits of sexual immorality, perversions, gross blasphemy, and unashamed mockery.

All these and other characteristics need to be observed with a discerning eye. Counsel with others is of great help at this point. Be cautious about making a premature diagnosis. A reliable Christian therapist can be helpful.

2. *There must be help provided to the demonized person.* If you become convinced that demons are, in fact, involved, the demonized person will need assistance from caring, strong Christians who will work together in relieving the victim of evil. A careful study of Jesus' procedure is urged. For example, He sought the name of the demon. He took charge and did not relinquish control.

He also commanded that the demon come out. It is never advisable that this process be attempted alone. There is strength in numbers . . . especially mature, discerning Christians. Such experiences can be extremely difficult and violent.

3. *There must be follow-up support after the ordeal.* A most vulnerable time occurs after the individual is relieved of demonism. A great deal of care and support is needed. Glance over Luke 11:24–26. It will help you see the value of follow-up.

> *When the unclean spirit goes out of a man, it passes through waterless places seeking rest, and not finding any, it says, "I will return to my house from which I came." And when it comes, it finds it swept and put in order. Then it goes and takes along seven other spirits more evil than itself, and they go in and live there; and the last state of that man becomes worse than the first.*

Do not leave the individual without your assistance.

SUMMARY AND CONCLUSION

We have covered a lot of territory in these few pages. We have discovered that in order for us to stand our ground and do battle victoriously against the powers of darkness, ignorance must be dispelled and the armor God has provided must be taken up and put on. We also determined that there are two basic ways the Bible teaches us to deal with demons: (1) to resist them, and (2) to cast them out. These truths have helped us realize that in Jesus Christ we are the victors, the conquerors. There is no need to be afraid. We have overcoming power through Him who died that we might live. Stand firm, Christian. Through Christ we conquer.

I can think of no more appropriate way to conclude these thoughts than to quote Revelation 12:11, a verse that says it all about our spiritual war with Satan.

> *And they overcame him because of the blood of the Lamb and because of the word of their testimony, and they did not love their life even to death.*

Almighty God and faithful Friend, You know the times in which we live are wicked, perverse, and increasingly more godless as every year passes. And it is so easy for us to become frightened, since we are surrounded by every evidence of gross evil. As your children, we are like an island of purity surrounded by a troubled dark sea of depravity . . . a place where satanic and demonic activity is happening.

On top of all that, we cannot see our real enemy. Therefore, we cannot reach out and fight him with our fists. But he is there, relentlessly and ruthlessly working against You and Your will. This frightens us, we freely admit. But we have learned that there is no reason to be afraid. Your armor is all we need. Your strength is our shield. Your presence is our confidence.

Convince us of this, O Lord. Reassure us that You are our light, our protection, and our shield. We need those reminders. Give them to us each day. May we stand firm in Your power as we find our strength in You rather than tremble before the enemy. Only through the blood of our Lord Jesus Christ do we conquer!

We pray in the all-conquering name of Your Son,
Amen.

CHAPTER ELEVEN

HOPE

Our bodies have been constructed to withstand an enormous amount of stress and pressure. God has made us to be fairly resilient people. We can survive the heat of the tropics or the icy winds of winter. With undaunted courage, we can go through seasons of illness, financial reversals, domestic disappointments, unemployment, or the death of someone dear to us . . . if. If we don't lose the one essential ingredient.

Hope.

We can rebound against wind and weather, calamity and tragedy, disease and death, so long as we have our hope. We can live weeks without food, days without water, and even several minutes without air, but take away our hope and within only a few seconds, we toss in the towel!

Knowing that is true about His creatures, God calls hope the "anchor of the soul," the irreplaceable, irreducible source of determination. He not only calls it our "anchor," He develops a helpful series of thoughts about hope in His Book, the Bible. But in one special section of Scripture, He concentrates direct attention upon this subject. That particular section is the major emphasis of this chapter.

If you find yourself wearing thin in hope or starting to wonder if you are going to be able to survive the things life is throwing at you, these next few pages may help.

Somewhere along our many miles of southern California shoreline walked a young, twenty-year-old woman with a terminal disease in her body and a revolver in her hand.

She had called me late one evening. We talked for a long time. A troubled young woman, her mind was filled with doubts. She had advanced leukemia. The doctors told her she would not live much longer. She checked herself out of a hospital because, as she put it, she "couldn't take another day of that terrible isolation."

Her husband had left her.

Her two-month-old daughter had recently died.

Her best friend had been killed in an auto accident.

Her life was broken. She'd run out of hope. I'll come back to this woman later on.

MAXIMUM PRESSURE POINTS

Doubts often steal into our lives like termites into a house. These termite-like thoughts eat away at our faith. Usually, we can hold up pretty well under this attack. But occasionally, when a strong gale comes along—a sudden, intense blast—we discover we cannot cope. Our house begins to lean. For some people it completely collapses. It is during these stormy times, during the dark days and nights of tragedy and calamity, that we begin to feel the destructive effects of our doubts—running like stress fractures through the structure of our lives.

For me, there are three times when the intensity of doubt reaches maximum proportions. One such time is when things I believe should never happen, occur.

There are times when my loving, gracious, merciful, kind, good, sovereign God surprises me by saying yes to something I was convinced He would say no to. When bad things happen to good people. When good things happen to bad people. When a lie is passed off as the truth and wins the hearing of the majority.

In his book *When Bad Things Happen to Good People*, Rabbi Harold Kushner writes:

> There is only one question which really matters: Why do bad things happen to good people? All other theological

conversation is intellectually diverting. . . . Virtually every
meaningful conversation I have ever had with people on
the subject of God and religion has either started with
this question, or gotten around to it before long.[1]

I once received a letter from a woman who heard a talk I had
given on a radio program, entitled, "Riding Out the Storm." Little
did she know how meaningful it would be to her. Just as she was
entering into the truth of that message, she arrived at home to discover that her young, recently married daughter had been brutally
murdered.

Why did God say yes to that? Why did that bad thing happen to that good person? The effect of such termites within our
soul is great. They eat away at us, and doubt wins a hearing.

Doubts also increase when things I believe should happen,
never occur (the other side of the coin). When I expected God to
say yes but He said no. Numerous parents of young men and
women have said good-bye and sent their children away to war,
convinced God would bring them home again. But sometimes He
says no. How about the family of the policeman who was killed at
the onion field outside Bakersfield? Think of their rage as they
went the distance to see that the murderers were finally sent to the
gas chamber—only to realize the inescapable fact that not only
were the killers allowed to live, but one would later be set free.

Joni Eareckson Tada (and a thousand like her) trust confidently for awhile that the paralysis will go away—that God will say,
"Yes, I'll get you through this. I'll teach you some deep lessons,
and then I will use you with full health in days to come as I heal you
completely." But God ultimately says no.

Evangelist Leighton Ford and his wife, Jean, members of the
Billy Graham Evangelistic Association team, lost their twenty-one-
year-old son, Sandy, some years ago. Four days after the funeral,
Ford spoke to the Graham team. His conversation was recorded in
part in an issue of *Decision* magazine:

A week ago yesterday, right before Thanksgiving, my
stomach was so tied up in knots, so anxious that I had to
get out and run. When I stopped, I prayed: I talked with

God. I said, "Lord, I know You can heal Sandy through
this surgery if You want to. If You don't want to, I can't
imagine why You don't." I can't tell you everything I was
feeling, but I remember that I finally prayed and said,
"God, I just want to say one thing, be good to my boy
tomorrow."

I am conscious that almost every one of us has
within our heart—some openly, some secretly—a great
gaping, grieving wound that we carry. And in the midst of
it we say, "Why? Is God really good?"[2]

That father wanted a yes answer to his prayers. Sandy died.
God said no. And Ford admits:

I would be less than honest if I did not tell you that I wish
I could just smile and say, "I'm thankful for this." For
there is a part of me inside that says, "It is not right." . . .
I say these things inside myself. They fight. There are
hours of great peace and joy, and then there are times
when it just closes in, and I say, ". . . Am I doubting
God?"[3]

When we expect Him to say yes and He says no, doubts
multiply.

There's a third situation where doubts grow. This takes place
when things that I believe should happen *now*, occur much, much
later. Of all the doubts which "rap and knock and enter in our soul"
(Browning), perhaps few are more devastating than those that happen when we are told by God, in effect. "Wait, wait, wait, wait . . .
wait . . . wait!" All of us have wrestled greatly with His timing.

These "pressure points" provide a perfect introduction to
the verses in Hebrews 6. This is that great chapter that begins with
a strong warning, continues with words of affirmation, and closes
with words of reassurance and ringing confidence. It addresses the
Christian hanging on by his fingernails as he feels himself sliding
down the hill. It shouts: "Persevere! Hang tough! Be strong! Don't
quit!" Even when God says no, and you expected yes. Even when

He says yes, and you anticipated no. And especially when He says to wait, and you expected it now.

A CLASSIC EXAMPLE: ABRAHAM

> ... *when God made the promise to Abraham, since He could swear by no one greater, He swore by Himself, saying, "I will surely bless you, and I will surely multiply you." And thus, having patiently waited, he obtained the promise (Hebrews 6:13–15).*

What's all that about? Well, maybe we should become acquainted with the warning that comes just before the mention of Abraham. Verse 12 says:

> ... *that you may not be sluggish, but imitators of those who through faith and patience inherit the promises.*

Imitate those strong-minded men and women in biblical history! They believed God. They said, in effect, "I will stand, no matter what occurs. I will believe God, even though my world crumbles and my house leans. No calamity will make me fall!"

As an illustration of just such an individual, Abraham is mentioned. Now if you don't know your Bible, you can't appreciate the extent to which Abraham and Sarah trusted God. The two of them had been married for years. She was sixty-five; he was seventy-five. And if you can believe this, God had said to the man that in the latter years of his life, his wife was going to have a baby. God promised Abraham in no uncertain terms; He swore on the basis of His own integrity that Sarah would have a son. Then, after making that firm promise, God said, "Now you trust Me. You wait."

Abraham waited a year, and nothing happened. By then, Sarah had turned sixty-six.

He waited another ten years, and by that time she was seventy-six. Still nothing had happened.

Another ten years—nothing at all.

Then, when Abraham was nearing his one hundredth birthday (which means his wife was about ninety years old), God came

back and said, "I'm here again. Guess what? You're still going to
have that baby."

If we were to return to the original time when the first dia-
logue occurred, we would gain a whole new appreciation for God's
faithfulness and consistency. It's a wonderful story because it proves
how trustworthy God is in the waiting period. Let's pick up the
narrative as God is speaking to His friend, Abraham:

> . . . *"As for Sarai your wife, you shall not call her name
> Sarai, but Sarah shall be her name. And I will bless her, and
> indeed I will give you a son by her. Then I will bless her, and
> she shall be a mother of nations; kings of peoples shall come
> from her. Then Abraham fell on his face and laughed . . .*
> (Genesis 17:15–17).

Can't you imagine Abraham's response? "Oh, I cannot
believe this. God, here You are talking about this baby who is going
to come into our home. Oh, God, how can it be? How can it be?"
I love the man's honesty. I wonder if he was smiling, maybe chuck-
ling, when he answered,

> . . . *"Will a child be born to a man one hundred years
> old? And will Sarah, who is ninety years old, bear a child? . . .*
> *Oh that Ishmael might live before Thee!"* (vv. 17–18).

"We have this other young man in our home, God. Have it
happen through him"—that makes a lot of sense! No, God had
not planned that the arrangement would be through Ishmael. See
verse 19:

> . . . *"No, but Sarah . . . shall bear you a son, and you
> shall call his name Isaac. . . ."*

The name Isaac means *laughter* in Hebrew. "You laugh at
Me; I'll laugh at you. I'll show you when that boy is born, that I
keep My word."

Now you might think Sarah is waiting in the wings just as
confident as she can be that it will be exactly as it was promised.
Better take a close look at the Genesis account: chapter 18, verses
9 through 12. Three men have come for a visit, bringing the mes-

sage from God to underscore what He had said earlier. Abraham is there; Sarah's listening through the tent-flap.

> . . . *"Where is Sarah your wife?" And he said, "Behold, in the tent." And he said, "I will surely return to you at this time next year; and behold, Sarah your wife shall have a son." And Sarah was listening at the tent door, which was behind him. . . . Sarah was past childbearing. And Sarah laughed to herself . . . (vv. 9–12).*

Ninety years old, why not? There's not much else to do but laugh at something like that, you know. After all, "I'm ninety years old, and I'm going to get pregnant? I'm going to bear a son? You gotta be kidding!"

On our way back to Hebrews 6, let's stop off at Romans 4. We can't fully appreciate Hebrews or Genesis without the Romans 4 passage sandwiched in between. Here's our friend Abraham who might have laughed on the outside, but down deep was obviously confident God could do it. Romans 4:18:

> *In hope against hope he believed. . . .*

There it is, friends. That's what Hebrews 6 is talking about. "In hope against hope." When it didn't make sense. When the physical body couldn't pull it off. When it seemed an utter impossibility:

> . . . *in order that he might become a father of many nations, according to that which had been spoken, "So shall your descendants be." And without becoming weak in faith he contemplated his own body, now as good as dead since he was about a hundred years old, and the deadness of Sarah's womb; yet, with respect to the promise of God, he did not waver in unbelief, but grew strong in faith, giving glory to God, and being fully assured that what He had promised, He was able also to perform (Romans 4:18–21).*

That's a clear illustration of faith. That's believing even when doubts attack. That's being confident that God knows what He is doing regardless of the waiting period. That's being just as firm when there's a ten-year period to wait as when there's only one year ahead. He hoped against hope:

> . . . *with respect to the promise of God, he did not waver in unbelief, but grew strong in faith, giving glory to God (v. 20).*

That's a very important part of this sentence. While you wait, you give Him glory. While you trust Him, you give Him glory. While you accept the fact that He has you in a holding pattern, you give Him glory.

> . . . *being fully assured that what He had promised, He was able also to perform. . . . It was reckoned to him as righteousness (vv. 21–22).*

The man walked patiently through those years, trusting God.

TRUSTING . . . IN SPITE OF THE CIRCUMSTANCES

Now back to Hebrews 6. This isn't a lesson on Abraham's life; this is a lesson for us today. It's a lesson on trusting God when things don't go our way; on how to deal with doubt; on having hope when the answers haven't come; on being confident in God when we cannot be confident in our circumstances or our future.

See the transition in verse 16? It all goes back to God's promising on His name that everything would occur just as He promised. Now to bring it into focus, men and women today, the writer adds:

> *[People today] swear by one greater than themselves, and with them an oath given as confirmation is an end of every dispute (v. 16).*

Right hand raised, "Do you swear to tell the truth, the whole truth, and nothing but the truth, so help you God?" You've sworn on One greater than your name, and you are expected in the courtroom to tell the truth. There was none greater, so Almighty God swore on His own name. The writer says in this transitional principle: "Men swear by calling on a name greater than their own name."

In biblical days, before the day of attorneys, title companies, and other modern institutions, people settled their disagreements by coming to a mutual understanding and then confirming it with a promise. Such an oath or promise was final in its authority and settled disputes.

In those days, there were many ways to signify you had negotiated an agreement: You shook hands, or you raised your hand, or you put your thigh next to the thigh of the other person, or you put your hand under the thigh of one who was aged—a number of things were done. But you would swear when you touched the other person that you would do such and such, exactly as you had promised, and it was an oath based on a name greater than your own. Abraham had a promise based on God's name; it wouldn't fail. What hope it must have given that old man!

Now, verse 17. Look at how it all ties in:

> *In the same way God, desiring even more to show to the heirs of the promise the unchangeableness of His purpose, interposed with an oath. . . .*

With God, there is an unchangeable purpose. It is mysterious. It is unfathomable. There is no way, in this point of time, we can unravel all of the reasons behind His purpose. But it is unchangeable; it is so firm He has confirmed it by an oath. The passage goes on to say:

> *. . . in order that by two unchangeable things, in which it is impossible for God to lie . . .*

The purpose He has planned for us and the oath He has taken, swearing that that purpose will be unchanged and ultimately right—those two things stand as God's confirmation to His people.

THE NEED TO THINK THEOLOGICALLY, NOT LOGICALLY

I confess to you, at times I doubt God's purpose and promise. I say that to my own embarrassment. When things haven't worked as I thought they would, when I received a no instead of a yes or a yes instead of a no, when I couldn't unravel a situation and fit it with the character of God . . . those have been times when I've said, "I know down inside this isn't right." The writer is coming to us on his knees, saying, "Please, rather than thinking logically, think theologically!" That's awfully good advice.

When the bottom drops out of your life, when hope starts to wear thin, when human logic fails to make much sense, think *theologically!* Go back and read Hebrews 6:17–18. The theological facts are: (1) there is an unchangeable purpose with God, and (2) that purpose is guaranteed with an oath.

It's at this juncture I should add: Don't try to explain it all to someone else. You can't. If you could, you would be God. The only thing you can explain theologically is that it is part of His unchangeable purpose, guaranteed with an oath, neither of which is a lie. That's theological thinking. As Solomon states so well: "[God] has made everything appropriate in its time" (Ecclesiastes 3:11a).

Let me give you a syllogism—a theological syllogism:

> *God is in control of the times and seasons.*
> *Some times are hard, and some seasons are dry.*

So the conclusion is:

> *God is in control of hard times and dry seasons.*

We are quick to give God praise when the blessings flow: when the checking account is full and running over; when the job is secure, and a promotion is on the horizon; when the salary is good; when our health is fine. But we have a tough time believing when those things aren't true.

THREE BENEFITS OF THINKING THEOLOGICALLY

There are benefits that come from thinking theologically; you'll see three of them right here in these two verses in Hebrews 6. Look at verse 18:

> . . . *by two unchangeable things, in which it is impossible for God to lie, we may have strong encouragement . . .*

Logical thinking will discourage you; theological thinking will encourage you. That's the first benefit . . . *personal encouragement*. Believe it. You will have "strong encouragement."

Read on:

> . . . *we who have fled for refuge in laying hold of the hope* . . .

That's the second benefit . . . *a refuge of hope*. Encouragement is the opposite of discouragement. Hope is the opposite of despair. When you accept the fact that sometimes seasons are dry and times are hard and that God is in control of both, you will discover a sense of divine refuge, because the hope then is in God and not in yourself. That explains why Abraham gave glory to God during the waiting period. "I can't figure it out. I cannot explain it, but Lord, You promised me . . . and I give You glory for the period of waiting, even though I'm getting up in years."

A strong encouragement, a refuge of hope, and for the ultimate benefit, read on:

> *This hope we have as an anchor of the soul* . . .

That's the third benefit . . . *an anchor for the soul*. The word *anchor* is used often in ancient literature, but it is only used once in the New Testament, right here in Hebrews 6. There are lots of hymns and gospel songs that make use of the anchor metaphor. Every one of them comes back to this verse that refers to the "anchor of the soul."

There's something beautiful in this word picture that I would have missed without the advice of one very capable scholar:

> The picture is that of an ancient sailing vessel finding its way through the narrow entrance to a harbor. This was one of the trickiest maneuvers the captain of a ship had to make. As his ship moved through the opening, he had to guard against a gust of wind running it onto a reef or a sandbar. The skeleton of many a ship could be seen on the rocks, giving testimony to the fact that its captain had failed his navigation test.

To minimize the risk, the olden-day skipper would lower the ship's anchor into a smaller boat, which would then be rowed through the narrow entrance of the harbor. The anchor would then be dropped and this ship, with sails down, would be pulled past the obstacles, through the narrow opening and into the safety of the harbor.[4]

I distinctly remember when our troop ship arrived (after seventeen days at sea!) at the port city of Yokohama, Japan. As we approached the harbor, the skipper stopped our ship, and it sat silent in the deep sea, like an enormous, bloated whale. We marines waited on the deck in the hot sunshine as a tiny tugboat left the harbor and came out toward our huge vessel. Soon, a small Japanese gentleman came up the side of our ship and ultimately took the controls of our ship as he personally guided it until we were safely docked in the harbor. Someone later explained the reason to me: There were still mines in the Japanese harbor. (That's a fun thought after seventeen days at sea: "Welcome to Japan; the mines are ready for you!") The Japanese man guided us through the treacherous waters of the harbor and brought us safely to the pier.

THE SPIRITUAL ANALOGY

The point of all of this, of course, is not anchors and skippers, ships and harbors. The point is this: That is exactly what Jesus Christ does when the bottom of life drops out. Look closely at the verse:

> . . . *We have as an anchor of the soul, a hope both sure and steadfast and one which enters within the veil (v. 19).*

The imagery of that verse may not be clear at first glance. Let me put it in today's terms. In the days of the Tabernacle, the Jews gathered around it and within it as a place of worship. Within the Tabernacle were veils; behind the innermost veil was the holiest place on earth, the place we might call the "God-room." In this God-room, the light (it was actually called the *shekinah*) of God resided. It's my understanding that the light of God was a brilliant, blazing radiance that shone down into the God-room. Within that room was an ark, or a small chest, much lower and smaller than most pulpits. On top of that chest was a grail, with golden cherubim on either end (angel-like creatures with their wings folded in front of them). That entire piece of unique furniture was too holy for words.

Once a year, the high priest of the Jews would enter that God-room with a small pan of blood which, precisely as God required it in the Law, he poured out on the grail (which was called the "mercy seat") there between the golden cherubim. God, witnessing the spilling of the blood and pleased with the sacrifice that had been made correctly by the priest, graciously forgave the Jewish people. It was an annual event, the most sacred of all events. The Hebrews must have held their breath as the high priest went in with the pan, poured the blood, and came out of this room where God dwelled. The first-century Jews who read this word *veil* in Hebrews 6 understood all that. Look closely:

> *This hope we have as an anchor . . . a hope both sure and steadfast . . . one which enters within the veil, where Jesus has entered as a forerunner for us, having become a high priest forever according to the order of Melchizedek (vv. 19–20).*

In other words, our Savior has gone through life, has taken all of life's beatings and buffetings, and has gone before us. And now? Now He pulls us toward Himself! He invites His followers within the veil. He says, "Come in. Find healing for your stress fractures. Find here the rest that you need, the relief from the burdens and buffetings of doubt."

Doubt, you see, will always try to convince you, *You are all alone. No one else knows. Or cares. No one else really can enter in and help you with this.* In Hebrews, however, the writer says that Christ is a constant priest—not once a year, but forever. He lives in the God-room. He is there, sitting alongside the Father, representing your needs to Him. And, child of God, there is nothing so great for you to endure that He does not feel touched by it and stay by you through it.

SOME PERTINENT AND PRACTICAL REMINDERS

Perhaps a practical warning should be stated here. When you minister to people who have come to the end of their trail of despair, *logic won't cut it*. Logical thinking will not help you, nor will it help them. Sometimes, quite honestly, it will backfire.

Writer Harriet Sarnoff Schiff has distilled her pain and tragedy in a book called *The Bereaved Parent*. She remembers that when her young son died during an operation to correct a congenital heart malfunction, her clergyman took her aside and said, "I know that this is a painful time for you. But I know that you will get through it all right, because God never sends us more of a burden than we can bear. God only let this happen to you because He knows that you are strong enough to handle it." Harriet Schiff remembers her reaction to those words: "If only I was a weaker person, Robbie would still be alive."[5]

Human logic breaks down in crisis. The mystery is enormous, and it is the enormity of it all that calls for faith. I'm sorry if that sounds like an overused bromide. But if we could unravel it, why would we need faith? If that were true, all we'd really need is the answer in the back of the book and someone to point it out to us; we'd read it, and that's all there would be to it. But God's plan is that we walk by faith, not by sight. It is faith and patience that stretch us to the breaking point. Such things send doubt running.

When you find yourself dealing with doubt, let me give you three things to remember. First, *God cannot lie*. He can test, and He will. He can say no, and He sometimes will; He can say yes, and He will; He can say wait, and occasionally He will—but God cannot lie. He must keep His word. Doubt says, "You fool, you're stupid to believe in a God who puts you through this." By faith, keep remembering that God cannot lie.

I appreciate very much the words of one survivor of Auschwitz:

It never occurred to me to question God's doings or lack of doings while I was an inmate of Auschwitz. Although, of course, I understand others did. I was no less or no more religious because of what the Nazis did to us, and I believe my faith in God was not undermined in the least. It never occurred to me to associate the calamity we were experiencing with God, to blame Him, or to believe in Him less, or cease believing in Him at all because He didn't come to our aid. God doesn't owe us that, or anything. We owe our lives to Him. If someone believes God is responsible for the death of six million because He didn't somehow do something to save them, he's got his thinking reversed. We owe God our lives for the few or many years we live. And we have the duty to worship Him and do as He commands. That's what we're here on earth for; to be in God's service and to do God's bidding.[6]

God cannot lie.

Here's the second piece of advice that helps me: *We will not lose.* Doubt says, "You lose if you trust God through this. You lose." If I read anything in this whole section of Hebrews 6, I read that in the mysterious manner of God's own timing, for some unexplainable and yet unchangeable purpose, those of us who trust Him ultimately win—because God ultimately wins.

There's a little chorus Christians love to sing. It is quiet and tender, yet tough and true:

> In His time, in His time,
> He makes all things beautiful
> In His time.
>
> Lord, please show me every day,
> As You're teaching me Your way,
> That You do just what You say,
> In Your time.[7]

God cannot lie. We will not lose. Your mate has walked away from you, an unfair departure—you will not lose, child of God. Your baby has been born and for some reason, it has been chosen to be one of those special persons on this earth. You will not lose. You've waited and waited, and you were convinced things would improve, yet things have only gotten worse—keep remembering, you will not lose. God swears on it with an oath that cannot change. You will not lose.

Third—and I guess it's the best of all—is that *our Lord Jesus does not leave.* To quote a verse from Scripture, He "sticks closer than a brother" (Proverbs 18:24).

> *. . . Jesus has entered as a forerunner for us, having become a high priest forever . . . (Hebrews 6:20).*

That means He is there at any time . . . and always.

Remember the young woman on the beach I mentioned at the beginning of this chapter? Remember her circumstances? Advanced leukemia, daughter dead, husband gone, greater debt than she could ever repay. She had checked herself out of a hospital, deciding that anything would be better than the isolation she was in as she endured that advanced stage of leukemia.

She and I spoke calmly and quietly about what was happening. I did a lot of listening. There were periods when there was silence on the phone for thirty to forty-five seconds. I didn't know where she was. I still don't know her full name. She spoke of taking her husband's revolver and going out on the beach to finish it all. She asked me a lot of questions about suicide.

In what seemed an inappropriate moment . . . I felt peace, a total absence of panic. I had no fear that she would hang up and take her life. I simply spoke very, very quietly about her future. I made no special promise that she would immediately be healed. I knew that she might not live much longer, as her doctors were talking to her in terms of a very few weeks—perhaps days. I spoke to her about Christ and the hope He could provide. After a sigh and with an ache that was obvious, she hung up.

Thirty minutes later my phone rang again. It was the same young woman. She had a friend who was a nurse, who used to come to our church in Fullerton, California. The nurse had given her a New Testament in which she had written my name and phone number and had said, "If you really are in deep need, I think he will understand." By the way, the nurse—her closest friend—was the one who had been killed in the auto accident. She had nothing to cling to from that friendship but memories and this Testament. She read from it.

I said, "What does that little Book say to you?"

"Well, I think the first part of it is biography and the last part is a group of letters that explain how to do what's in that biography." (That's a good analysis of the New Testament.)

I said, "Have you done that?" And she had called back to say, "Yes, I've done that. I decided, Chuck, that I would, without reservation, give myself to Jesus Christ. I'm still afraid; I still have doubts. I still don't know what tomorrow's going to bring, but I want you to know that I have turned my life over to Jesus, and I'm trusting Him through this. He has given me new hope . . . the one thing I really needed."

It's very possible that someone reading these words right now feels the very same way. You're thinking thoughts that you have never entertained before, and you're thinking them more often and more seriously. Without trying to use any of the clichés on you, I would say that this hope Christ can bring, this "anchor of the soul," is the only way through. I have no answer other than Jesus Christ. I can't promise you healing, nor can I predict that your world will come back right side up. But I *can* promise you He will receive you as you come in faith to Him. And He will bring back the hope you need so desperately. The good news is this: That hope will not only get you through this particular trial, it will ultimately take you "within the veil" when you die.

Father, it is my desire to give You praise even when bad things happen to good people. Even when the end seems terribly premature. And when I hear a no though I expected a yes . . . or a yes when I was so sure of a no . . . or "wait" when I was confident of "now." When the doubts storm in to blight my faith and tempt me to question Your integrity, help me, Father! Only You can do that, like You did for Abraham and Sarah, who waited twenty-five long years for the fulfill-

ment of a single promise. Help us not to stagger in unbelief but, like Abraham, to trust You through times of doubt.

In the name of Christ, the Giver of hope, our permanent and powerful Priest, I pray,

Amen.

CHAPTER TWELVE

GOD'S WILL

For too many years Christians have relied on vague hunches and weird hocus-pocus to know God's will. The paths that lead to an understanding of His plan are strewn with the litter of confusion, mystery, frustration, guilt, superstition . . . and major stress fractures!

Long enough.

God isn't playing a guessing game with His people. His will for us is neither puzzling nor hidden within some deep, dark cave requiring magical words to let us in on the secret. No, nothing like that at all. He wants us to know and to do His will; therefore, He is actively engaged in the process of revealing it. Contrary to popular opinion, anyone who sincerely seeks His will can find it.

Admittedly, there are a few biblical insights that help clarify the will of God. That's the purpose of this chapter. Within these pages you will read plain and uncomplicated words that will give the assistance you need to pursue God's will for your life. Because everything in these pages rests firmly on scriptural foundations, you can rely on this counsel without fear of being misled. Who knows? The next few pages could include the answers you need that will help put your life on target— something you've been wanting for years.

I certainly hope so.

t is a riddle wrapped in a mystery inside an enigma."

That's the way the late Sir Winston Churchill once described the actions of Russia. That is also the way many would describe the will of God. As a result, all kinds of approaches and techniques are used to decipher the secret code. Some are so ridiculous, they make us shake our heads in disbelief. If they were not employed with such sincerity and devotion, they would be downright hilarious.

SOME UNBELIEVABLE METHODS

If we were looking for a new television series to amuse and entertain, we could name this one "That's Unbelievable!" Here are some examples we could feature on the show.

- A lady received a brochure advertising a tour to Israel. Because going to the Holy Land was one of her lifelong dreams, she really wanted to go. She had the money, the time, the interest, and the strength. But was it God's will? Before going to bed, she read the pamphlet once more and noticed that the airplane they would be traveling on was a 747 jumbo jet. After spending a sleepless night wrestling with all the pros and cons, she was greatly relieved the following morning. She now knew it was God's will for her to go. How did she know for sure? When she awoke and glanced at her digital clock, it read 7:47. That was her "sign" from God.

Now, that's unbelievable!

- A collegian needed a car. He didn't know which one God would have him purchase, but as a Christian, he was determined to find God's will before he bought anything. One night, he had a series of dreams. Everything in his dreams was yellow. He had his answer. After checking out several used car lots the next day, he finally found the one he was sure the Lord would have him buy. You guessed it. Yellow inside and out. He didn't bother to check it out. He didn't even give it a trial run around the block. It was yellow, so he bought it.

Appropriately, it turned out to be a lemon.

- A pastor had served as a deacon in a former church prior to being called into the ministry. He toyed with the idea of buying a doctor of divinity degree from a degree mill. He really wanted that degree, but he struggled with whether or not it was God's will. Late one afternoon, he stumbled across the answer he'd been looking for. Because it was in the Bible, all doubt was removed. The Lord had confirmed the minister's desire through 1 Timothy 3:13. The King James Version reads: "For they that have used the office of a deacon well purchase to themselves a good degree . . ."

Now, friends and neighbors, *that's* unbelievable!

And who hasn't heard about (and tried!) "putting out a fleece" to find God's will?

- Like the woman who had been trying to discover God's will on a particular decision that was almost impossible to determine. Finally, she boiled it down to one of two options. Then came the "fleece." As she drove down the street, she told the Lord, "If it is Your will that I choose Option A, then keep the light at the next corner green until I get there."
- A similar situation was handled by one man in another manner. His "fleece" was the telephone. He bargained with God, "If it's Your will, then cause my phone to ring at 10:21 tonight."
- I heard recently of a young Christian struggling with the choice of his career. As he was driving and praying in Washington, D.C., he ran out of gas in front of the Philippine embassy. He got his answer. God wanted him to be a missionary and serve the Lord in the Philippines.

I wonder what this young man would do if he found himself suddenly stuck in an elevator with a young single woman named Mary. Would that be God's "sign" to marry her?

- And what about the Christian who sat by a window with his Bible open and allowed the wind to whip the pages over as he picked out a "verse for the day" to claim. His finger fell at random on the words "Judas went and hanged himself." Bewildered and shocked, he tried again and landed on "Go and do thou likewise." Further dismayed, he quickly tried a third time as the wind-and-finger method led him to "Whatsoever thou doest, do quickly."

"Ridiculous!" you say. Of course it is. And so are all these other strange approaches to determining God's will. Yet we've hardly scratched the surface of the wild and weird methods well-meaning people use to find His will. It happens every day, among people just like you and me who sincerely want to know the will of God.

SOME GENUINE CONCERNS

Lest we oversimplify the problem, let's understand that there are some legitimate areas of concern that aren't specifically addressed in the Bible. And intelligent, caring, genuine people in God's family are often at a loss to know what He would have them do.

- A high school senior plays outstanding basketball. He is in great demand. He can attend his choice of a dozen or more excellent universities, each offering a full scholarship. Which one is God's will for the Christian athlete?
- A single, happy, well-educated young woman has a good job and a hassle-free lifestyle. But to her surprise, she has recently found herself attracted to several young men at her church—all are believers as she is. Should she start thinking seriously about marriage? If so, which one would be God's choice for her?
- A family is living in southern California. They have numerous friends, a good church, a nice home, and family roots nearby. But Mom and Dad are starting to hate the smog more and more. The hurried pace, mixed with heavy traffic and too many people, is starting to take the

fun out of life. They want to move—but is it God's will? If it is, *where* would He have them live?

- A Christian couple has two children. He wants one or two more. She feels that two are about all she can handle. Both think they know God's will. Which one is right?

On top of these very real dilemmas, we read in the New Testament: "So then do not be foolish, but understand what the will of the Lord is" (Ephesians 5:17).

Such verses prod us off the fence of indecision, yet we are anxious not to do something "foolish" in the process. Even when our heart is right and our motive is pure, the will of God is not always set forth in a crystal clear manner, which intensifies our stress.

GOD'S DETERMINED WILL

Maybe it will help if we divide the subject into two parts. Think first of God's will as that which He has determined will occur. The Bible teaches us that God has a predetermined plan for every life. It is inevitable, unconditional, irresistible, and fixed. It includes and involves everything, such as our circumstances, decisions, achievements, failures, joys and sorrows, sufferings and sins, blessings and calamities, birth and death. Read the following scripture:

> *Blessed be the God and Father of our Lord Jesus Christ, who has blessed us with every spiritual blessing in the heavenly places in Christ, just as He chose us in Him before the foundation of the world, that we should be holy and blameless before Him. In love He predestined us to adoption as sons through Jesus Christ to Himself, according to the kind intention of His will, to the praise of the glory of His grace, which He freely bestowed on us in the Beloved. In Him we have redemption through His blood, the forgiveness of our trespasses, according to the riches of His grace, which He lavished upon us. In all wisdom and insight He made known to us the mystery of His will, according to His kind intention which He purposed in Him with a view to an administration suitable to the fulness*

of the times, that is, the summing up of all things in Christ, things in the heavens and things upon the earth. In Him also we have obtained an inheritance, having been predestined according to His purpose who works all things after the counsel of His will, to the end that we who were the first to hope in Christ should be to the praise of His glory. In Him, you also, after listening to the message of truth, the gospel of your salvation—having also believed, you were sealed in Him with the Holy Spirit of promise, who is given as a pledge of our inheritance, with a view to the redemption of God's own possession, to the praise of His glory (Ephesians 1:3–14).

That says at length what Daniel 4:35 says in brief:

And all the inhabitants of the earth are accounted as nothing. But He does according to His will in the host of heaven and among the inhabitants of earth; and no one can ward off His hand or say to Him, "What hast Thou done?"

God, our sovereign and immutable Master, openly declares that life is no will-o'-the-wisp encounter with luck. His determined will is *being* accomplished free of frustration. The plan is comprehensive in scope and complete down to the tiniest detail. And it is *all* for His glory. Rather than causing us to fear, this truth is designed to put us at ease and calm our anxieties.

But what about sin? Was sin a part of God's determined will? Yes, it was. It neither shocked nor frustrated our eternal God when sin occurred in the Garden of Eden. His eternal plan included the sacrificial death of His Son for *sinful* man. Read for yourself 1 Peter 1:18–21, Acts 2:23, Luke 22:22. Christ's payment for our sin was no divine afterthought.

But doesn't this make God responsible for sin? No, in no way.

Let no one say when he is tempted, "I am being tempted by God"; for God cannot be tempted by evil, and He Himself does not tempt anyone. But each one is tempted when he is carried away and enticed by his own lust. Then when lust has conceived, it gives birth to sin; and when sin is accomplished, it brings forth death (James 1:13–15).

The Scripture never points a finger of blame at God regarding sin. When we humans commit sin, it is a human responsibility.

> *O Jerusalem, Jerusalem, who kills the prophets and stones those who are sent to her! How often I wanted to gather your children together, the way a hen gathers her chicks under her wings, and you were unwilling (Matthew 23:37).*

GOD'S DESIRED WILL

That last verse helps us see that there is another side of the coin. The Lord Jesus Christ declared with a heavy heart that He often wanted to gather the citizens of Jerusalem around Him, but they resisted and refused. His "desire" was to meet with them and have them respond positively to His offer of love, but they were "unwilling."

Back again into Ephesians 5, we are told not to be unwise (v. 15). That's God's desired will for us. But how often we resist His desire! We are told not to be foolish (v. 17) or to get drunk (v. 18). That is His desire, but it isn't always what happens. He tells husbands to love their wives (v. 25). But the decision to obey is the husband's to make. You see, God's desired will calls for a human response—which leaves room for His desire not to be fulfilled. A simple chart will help:

Determined Will	*Desired Will*
Predestined	Calls for our cooperation
Comprehensive, eternal	Limited, temporal
It will occur	It may or may not occur
Cannot be frustrated	It can be resisted
Emphasis: God's sovereignty	Emphasis: Man's responsibility
Purpose: To glorify God	Purpose: To glorify God

Some of my ultra-Calvinistic friends who struggle as they read this will say, "But haven't you read Psalm 32:8?"

> *I will instruct you and teach you in the way which you should go; I will counsel you with My eye upon you.*

"Clearly, God takes full responsibility," they assert. "He promises to instruct, to teach, to lead us in *the* way . . . and that means it is *all* up to Him!" they add. Yes, I have read that verse, but I have also read the verse that follows, which warns me, "Do not be as the horse or as the mule . . ." You see, His desire for us to obey His leading can be blocked if we fail to cooperate, like a self-willed horse or a stubborn mule.

Many who discover these two sides to the will of God often want to know if it is possible for us to know His determined will. My friend, author J. Grant Howard, answers that quite well.

> Can I know the determined will of God for my life? Yes—after it has occurred! You now know that God's determined will for your life was that you be born of certain parents, in a certain location, under certain conditions, and that you be male or female. You now know that God determined for you to have certain features, certain experiences, certain teachers, certain interests, certain friends, a certain kind of education, and certain brothers and/or sisters, or perhaps to be an only child. In other words, everything that has happened in your life to this moment has been part of God's determined will for your life. It has happened because He has determined it to be so.
>
> What about the future? Can I know any part of God's determined will for my life in the future? Your spiritual position and eternal destiny are the only two things you can know with certainty. If you are in Christ now, you can know for certain that you will remain in Christ at every moment in the future (John 5:24, 10:27–29; Romans 5:1; 2 Corinthians 5:17). If you are not a Christian, you are in sin right now and you can know for certain that you will remain in that spiritually dead position in the future unless and until you personally receive Christ as your Savior (Ephesians 2:1–3). . . .
>
> The remainder of your future is hidden from you until it happens. Your career, marriage partner, home location, grades in school, friends, sicknesses, accidents,

honors, travels, income, retirement, etc., are all a part of
God's determined will but are not revealed to you ahead
of time . . .

What should be the Christian's attitude toward the
determined will of God? He should recognize it as a reality—clearly taught in the Word of God. Rest in it as
good, because that's what God says about it—He causes
all things to work together for good to those who love
Him (Romans 8:28). Beyond that, don't worry about it
and don't try to figure it out, because His ways are
unfathomable (Romans 11:33).[1]

Having come to terms with this clarification, we are now able
to pursue the solution to two crucial issues: How does God make
His will known? And how can I know if I am in His will?

HOW DOES GOD MAKE HIS WILL KNOWN?

Because this is only a brief chapter, I cannot get into all
phases of the subject, so I must assume several things.

1. I'll assume you are fairly healthy, physically and emotionally. If not, it is doubtful you can correctly follow the guidelines
I'm going to suggest with the level of sensitivity needed for such a
pursuit. Poor health tends to create a mental or emotional fog in
the process of interpreting God's will.

2. I'll assume you really want to know His will. Unless this is
true, numerous problems are created that again block a proper flow
of understanding.

3. I'll assume you are willing to adapt, change, and flex if you
discover such is needed. Obedience is essential. Doing God's will
is the flip side of discovering it.

4. I'll assume you are a Christian, one who knows God personally through faith in His Son. This is "family truth" that can be
applied by family members only.

Now then, let me ask you to stop, look, and listen. God
makes His desires known to those who stop at His Word, look in
with a sensitive spirit, and listen to others. When we go to His
Word, we stop long enough to hear from above. When we look, we

examine our surrounding circumstances in light of what He is say-ing to our inner spirit (perhaps you prefer to call this your con-science). And when we listen to others, we seek the counsel of wise, qualified people.

Stop at the Scriptures

The Bible tells us that the entrance of God's Word gives light (Psalm 119:130). That it is a lamp for our feet and a light that shines brightly on our path (Psalm 119:105). God has placed His Word in our hands and allowed it to be translated into our tongue (both were His *determined will*) so we could have a much more objective set of guidelines to follow than dreams, digital clock read-ings, hunches, impulses, and feelings. Sixty-six books filled with precepts and principles. And the better we know His Word, the more clearly we will know His will.

Precepts. Some of the statements that appear in the Bible are specific, black-and-white truths that take all the guesswork out of the way. Here are a few:

> *For this is the will of God, your sanctification; that is, that you abstain from sexual immorality (1 Thessalonians 4:3).*

As we saw in chapters 5 and 6, sexual immorality is never the will of God.

> *See that no one repays another with evil for evil, but always seek after that which is good for one another and for all men. Rejoice always; pray without ceasing; in everything give thanks; for this is God's will for you in Christ Jesus (1 Thessalonians 5:15–18).*

These specific things are stated to be the will of God. There are even times that suffering is directly the will of God for us.

First Corinthians 7 says a lot about remaining single as well as being committed to one's marriage. Clearly, this chapter (along with 2 Corinthians 6:14) states that a Christian is definitely not to marry a non-Christian. These are finely tuned *precepts* that reveal God's will.

Principles. But the Bible also has principles, general guidelines to assist us through the gray areas. Not so much "do this" and "don't do that," but an appeal to use wisdom and discretion when such are needed.

We have both precepts and principles in our traffic laws. The sign that reads "Speed Limit 35" is a precept. The one that reads "Drive Carefully" is a principle. And that principle will mean one thing on a deserted street at two o'clock in the morning, but something else entirely at three-thirty in the afternoon when children are walking home from school.

Just remember this: A primary purpose of the Word of God is to help us know the will of God. Become a careful, diligent student of Scripture. Those who are will be better equipped to understand His desires and walk in them.

Look Around and Within

Philippians 2:12–13 presents a good cause for our cooperating with the Lord's leading:

> *So then, my beloved, just as you have always obeyed, not as in my presence only, but now much more in my absence, work out your salvation with fear and trembling; for it is God who is at work in you, both to will and to work for His good pleasure.*

These verses highlight three specifics: There's a willingness to obey. There's the need to "work out" or give ourselves to doing our part with a sensitive spirit (fear and trembling). And then there's the promise that God will "work in you" to accomplish His plan. As we remain alert to His working, paying close attention to doors He opens and closes, He directs us into His will.

This reminds me of Paul on the second missionary journey. He crossed the vast country we know today as Turkey, hoping and trying to preach the gospel. Yet one door after another slammed in his face (read Acts 16:6–10). Finally, on the western-most edge of the country, at the town named Troas, God announced to him that He wanted Paul to go farther west into Europe and proclaim the truth over there. An open door awaited him.

Closed doors are just as much God's leading as open ones. The believer who wants to do God's will *must* remain sensitive and cooperative, not forcing his way into areas that God closes off. The Lord uses circumstances and expects us to "read" them with a sensitive, alert conscience.

We *must* stop and check His Word. We must look around and within. And there is one more helpful piece of advice to remember. We *must* . . .

Listen to the Counsel of Qualified People

Solomon the wise once wrote:

> *A plan in the heart of a man is like deep water, but a man of understanding draws it out (Proverbs 20:5).*

> *Iron sharpens iron, so one man sharpens another. . . . As in water face reflects face, so the heart of man reflects man (Proverbs 27:17, 19).*

As we read earlier, Jethro, Moses' father-in-law, gave him good counsel when he challenged him to delegate his work load (Exodus 18). Older women in God's family are told to instruct and encourage the younger women (Titus 2:3–5). Colossians 3:16 and Romans 15:14 exhort Christians to counsel and admonish each other. It is a great help to have the wise, seasoned, objective insights of those who are mature in the faith.

Like a quarterback, facing fourth-and-one on the thirty-yard line, who calls a time-out to consult with the coach, so must we. God uses others to help us know His desires.

God makes His will known: (1) through His Word . . . as we stop and study it, (2) through circumstances . . . as we look within and sense what He is saying, and (3) through the counsel of others . . . as we listen carefully.

HOW CAN I KNOW I AM IN GOD'S WILL?

God *wants* us to know and do His will. He consistently and diligently works on our behalf to assure and affirm us. He gives us two specific go-ahead signals within to help us know we are fulfilling His desires.

Peace

> *And let the peace of Christ rule in your hearts, to which indeed you were called in one body; and be thankful (Colossians 3:15).*

Peace literally "acts as umpire" within us. We become increasingly more assured deep down inside. In the words of Romans 14:5, we become "fully convinced" in our own minds.

Satisfaction

In addition to peace, there is an abiding pleasure and satisfaction. We love doing it. Lots of internal itches are scratched. This explains why some who could make much more money in another profession stay in the ranks of teaching. Or why some endure the pressure of a certain calling year after year without seriously considering a change to something easier.

Sir Flinders Petrie, the father of Palestinian archaeology, once wrote a friend who questioned his motive for doing what he was doing. Part of the letter aptly illustrates the level of satisfaction God can give:

> "You seem to take for granted that as I am not working for money . . . I must therefore be working for fame," he said. "But would you be surprised to hear that this is not my mainspring? . . . I work because I can do what I am doing, better than I can do anything else . . . And I am aware that such work is what I am best fitted for. If credit of any sort comes from such work, I have no objection of any sort to it; but it is not what stirs me to work at all. I believe that I should do just the same in quantity and quality if all that I did was published in someone else's name.[2]

SOME OFTEN-ASKED QUESTIONS

There are several questions people often ask regarding God's will. Let's consider four of the more common ones.

1. *What if I know the will of God but deliberately do not do it?* Unhappily, this does occur. Imperfect human beings are, at times, openly disobedient. What happens on those occasions? As in every area of life, when we don't play by the rules, we must pay the consequences. But consequences don't usually happen immediately. In fact, for a temporary period of time, things may run along smoothly. Hebrews 11:25 mentions enjoying the passing pleasures of sin. Sin offers its pleasures . . . but they are short-lived.

Remember Jonah? He bought a ticket on the ship leaving for Tarshish and was even able to fall asleep. But by and by, he found himself in a threatening storm and finally in the belly of the fish. God brings discipline upon His children. This includes external consequences as well as internal conflicts. Guilt and heartache rage within. If you question that, check out David's words in Psalm 32:3–4. After his disobedience connected with the Bathsheba affair, the man admits maximum misery within.

On top of all this, there can be public embarrassment and shame as fellow Christians in the body of Christ experience the impact of your disobedience. When necessary discipline must be administered by the church (Matthew 18:15–17), the transgression you tried to keep secret becomes public knowledge. Your family also suffers. We are not isolated individuals. Like dominoes standing on end, when one falls, others are affected.

2. *Can't I rely on my feelings?* This is frequently asked with regard to things we really want to do—but which lack biblical support. Take the case of a young woman madly in love with the man of her dreams. She is a Christian, but he is not. Of course, he promises he will be "everything a husband ought to be." He will not interfere with her interest in the Lord. She can trust him to give her plenty of space to attend church, have Christian friends—whatever. She just knows he is the one! With all her heart, she believes he will someday change. He will become a Christian, she is confident, after they get married. How does she think it's God's

will? Her feelings. This man makes her *feel* so good. He's the kind of guy she's always wanted.

But the Bible states unequivocally that to be unequally yoked with an unbeliever is NOT God's will, her feelings notwithstanding. Second Corinthians 6:14–18 and 1 Corinthians 7:39 are not eased by warm feelings and romantic moonlit nights. No matter how strong our feelings may be, when there are biblical precepts and/or principles that point us in a certain direction, we dare not ignore or disobey God's Word.

3. *Can I be in the will of God and not know it?* Yes, indeed. In fact, I'm of the opinion many Christians are! While it is true God desires us to be "filled with the knowledge of His will" (Colossians 1:9), many believers are not at that level of awareness. Furthermore, there is the weird yet popular idea that God's will is always something uncomfortable, painful, or unfulfilling. To some, it is inconceivable that God's will could be enjoyable—even delightful. Romans 12:2 states very clearly that His will is ". . . good and acceptable and perfect." Yes, we can say and do certain things that are in harmony with God's will and yet not be aware of it.

Quite honestly, we can cultivate certain habits that are pleasing to Him and consistently carry them out without even thinking about their being His will. This would include things like cultivating good personal relationships, keeping short accounts with sin, paying our bills promptly, maintaining a healthy body through a nutritious diet and sufficient exercise, and reacting correctly to stress.

4. *What about specifics that aren't addressed in Scripture?* The Bible doesn't tell the Christian specifically where to live. Or which career to pursue. Or where to go to college. If it did, how easy it would be. Yet how little faith we would need! That would reduce the Bible to a vocational guidance handbook, nothing more than a divinely inspired telephone directory . . . and just about as interesting. Our spiritual maturity would be no deeper than a third-grader's.

As I mentioned earlier in this chapter, God gives us principles. He also moves and works through circumstances. He even "speaks" to us through the wise counsel of a friend. All of this keeps us trusting, depending, waiting, praying, reading His Word, and using healthy doses of common sense.

The emphasis in Scripture is on who a person is and what a person does rather than on where a person lives. I have a family in mind who recently moved from southern California to Washington. Some very close friends of theirs really wanted to move with them, but had no leading from God that it was His will. Couple "A" has a child whose health is endangered by living in this area. As loving parents responding to the needs of their child, they packed up and left. Couple "B" has three children—healthy and happy—and are deeply involved in a discipleship ministry. For them to leave right now (even though they genuinely want to) would not be God's will. They have no peace in their hearts when they think seriously about joining their friends in Washington.

If the Lord wants you to get a specific message and to respond in an explicit manner, He has dozens of ways to communicate that to you. No mumbo-jumbo, no skywriting, no magic tricks or middle-of-the-night voices need to be sought. Those who really want to do His will, will know it (John 7:17).

Let me add this final piece of advice I often employ. When someone is convinced God is leading him or her in a specific direction, but you are not so convinced—yet you haven't a particular precept or principle from the Bible to point out why you disagree—learn a lesson from Paul's friends in Acts 21. The apostle was absolutely determined to go to Jerusalem, even though he knew danger lurked at every turn. Equally convinced to the contrary, a group of Christian friends (including his physician companion, Dr. Luke) attempted to change his plans. Unsuccessful, they backed off out of respect. Verse 14 says it all:

> *And since he would not be persuaded, we fell silent, remarking, "The will of the Lord be done!"*

Each believer is independently accountable to God for his or her response to the Lord's specific leading, even though others don't understand or agree.

THE MOST SATISFYING EXPERIENCE IN LIFE

No, finding God's will is not magical or mysterious. He hasn't hidden it in a digital clock or wrapped it in a complex riddle that calls for open windows or dreams and traffic lights to solve. Those who follow those methods are prime candidates for stress fractures. He has given us all we need to know it: His Book, daily circumstances, His Holy Spirit to communicate with our inner spirit, and wise friends and counselors. As I stated earlier, I'm convinced many are in His will who think they are not, because they are so fulfilled and happy in life. Surprising to some, God's will is the most satisfying experience in all of life.

* * *

Dear Father, I am grateful for the clear, unmistakable way Your Word communicates Your truth. Your will is not something to fear, but rather to accept and enjoy . . . because it is for our good and Your glory.

Thank You for clearing the fog of misunderstanding so that we can see and grasp the significance of this all important subject. Tenderly yet firmly, work with us so that we don't drift from the nucleus of Your will, which is really the safest place to be on the face of this earth. And the most fulfilling.

In the matchless name of Your Son,
Amen.

CHAPTER THIRTEEN

LIFE ASSURANCE

I've chosen to wrap up this book on stress fractures with one of the most encouraging, liberating truths in God's Word. I assure you, in all of life, there is no greater remedy for stress than a firm belief in the precious truth I will outline on the last few pages of this book.

Ironically, few subjects have created more disturbance (and stress!) in the Body of Christ than this very issue.

Simply stated, this is the question:

Can a Christian ever lose his or her salvation? Amplified, the larger question would be:

Once a person has been born again into the family of God—received new life, a new nature, been justified and sealed by the Holy Spirit—can that individual ever become unsaved by sinning, by ceasing to believe, or by any other cause?

In our fast-paced world of empty words, carnality, and shallow faith, not to mention the growing number of religious charlatans and defectors, the question becomes all the more important.

This final chapter is a brief yet potent statement worth your serious consideration. Because of its size, some things had to be omitted, but none of the vital ingredients of the issue are missing. In clear, uncomplicated terms, I have attempted to explain a doctrine that has been twisted and abused. Free from ridiculous, unbalanced extremes, these words offer you a reassuring, calm, and quiet confidence that you are absolutely secure in the everlasting arms of your eternal Savior.

In Him, you are safe!

L ucy and Linus, famous little people in Charles Schulz's car-
     toon "Peanuts," are staring out the window. The rain is
     pouring down.

Lucy speaks: "Boy, look at it rain! What if it floods the whole world?"

Linus answers: "It will never do that. In the ninth chapter of Genesis, God promised Noah that would never happen again, and the sign of the promise is the rainbow."

Lucy is looking directly at him as he is speaking. She turns back toward the window, smiles big, and announces: "You've taken a great load off my mind."

Linus responds: "Sound theology has a way of doing that!"

Wise and timely words from little Linus. With feelings of fear and uncertainty while watching events from our windows, many of us often hear least what we need most: sound, reliable theology that offers reassurance and hope, based squarely on God's Word. Not feelings or opinions or even logic. We need to hear what God has said and rest our case there.

As we think through the issues of the eternal security of the believer, our desire is to let God speak to us from the Scriptures. In doing so, most of our questions will be answered, and our struggles will begin to cease. But at the outset, let me encourage you to set aside all your defenses and relax your grip on any preconceived notions. To borrow from Lucy's response to Linus, God is ready to "take a great load off your mind" if you will simply accept what He declares.

THREE CRUCIAL FACTORS ABOUT SALVATION

As I ponder this subject, there are three crucial factors that impact the question, "Can a Christian ever lose his or her salvation?"

1. *We have in mind an individual who is truly born again;* one who possesses eternal life through faith in God's Son, the Lord Jesus Christ. Possessors, not professors.

Nowhere in Scripture does God promise eternal life to peo-ple who have done religious things, but have never truly accepted the gift of eternal life, having changed their minds from the rejection of Christ to faith in Him. No hand-raising, no walking down an aisle, no prayer, no church membership or baptism or sacrificial act or giving of money or attending evangelistic crusades will ever take the place of being born again. People who actually possess eternal life are directly linked by faith to Jesus, the Christ. Personally and deliberately, they have believed that Jesus died and rose from the dead for them.

Listen to the truth:

> *And the witness is this, that God has given us eternal life, and this life is in His Son. He who has the Son has the life; he who does not have the Son of God does not have the life (1 John 5:11–12).*

> *He saved us, not on the basis of deeds which we have done in righteousness, but according to His mercy, by the washing of regeneration and renewing by the Holy Spirit, whom He poured out upon us richly through Jesus Christ our Savior, that being justified by His grace we might be made heirs according to the hope of eternal life (Titus 3:5–7).*

> *For by grace you have been saved through faith; and that not of yourselves, it is the gift of God; not as a result of works, that no one should boast (Ephesians 2:8–9).*

Familiar words, but seldom taken *literally*. The person we are considering in this final chapter is truly and absolutely a child of God.

2. *The subject is eternal security, not temporal carnality.* We are not dealing with God's disciplining His wayward children.

If you mix these two subjects, you'll be hopelessly confused. Carnality has to do with the believer who willfully lives in the flesh and chooses a lifestyle that lacks the power and control of the Holy Spirit. If you will pause long enough to read three New Testament passages (1 Corinthians 3:1–3, Galatians 5:16–23, Hebrews 12:5–13), you'll see that a carnal Christian is a child of God who lives under the discipline of the Lord. Those scriptures do not refer to a Christian who has lost his salvation, but rather to one who has become wayward, one who is walking in the energy of the flesh.

Interestingly, those who teach that a Christian is not eternally secure usually have no place in their theology for carnality—and yet the Scriptures clearly set forth the sad but real fact that a child of God can slump into periods of "walking in the flesh." But as is true of children in our own family, they are still our children even if they willfully disobey us. We discipline them, but we cannot ever say they are not our children. Let's not confuse eternal security with temporary carnality.

3. *We must focus on what God has done for His children, not what we have done for Him.* This is foundational. Salvation is not something we earn, but rather something we receive as a gift. We did not pursue God. He pursued us. He came to our rescue when we were without righteousness, without a hint of hope within ourselves.

> *But God demonstrates His own love toward us, in that while we were yet sinners, Christ died for us (Romans 5:8).*

> *And you were dead in your trespasses and sins, in which you formerly walked according to the course of this world, according to the prince of the power of the air, of the spirit that is now working in the sons of disobedience. Among them we too all formerly lived in the lusts of our flesh, indulging the desires of the flesh and of the mind, and were by nature children of wrath, even as the rest. But God, being rich in mercy, because of His great love with which He loved us, even when we were dead in our transgressions, made us alive together with Christ (by grace you have been saved), and raised us up with Him, and seated us with Him in the heavenly places, in Christ Jesus, in order that in the ages to come He might show the surpassing riches of His grace in kindness toward us in Christ Jesus (Ephesians 2:1–7).*

When did our salvation occur? Look again at Romans 5:8—"while we were yet sinners." And, according to Ephesians 2, when we were spiritually "dead." When "we were by nature children of wrath."

Without wanting to be overbearing, I believe this must be the starting point for an understanding of eternal security. Since salvation is not something we earn or win, since it is not something we achieved by hard work, then it stands to reason that we ourselves cannot take it away. Salvation is God's gift. It is His power that makes it possible . . . and it is unthinkable and impossible for you and me to alter in any way the ultimate accomplishment of His plan.

QUESTION: CAN THE WORK OF GOD BE UNDONE?

Please consider the following statement very carefully. I'd like you to read it twice. The first time slowly, to yourself. The second time, aloud.

> **Since my security depends on what God has done for me through Christ, then various works of God would have to be undone or reversed if I could lose my salvation . . . and the Bible would certainly declare it.**

Before reading any further, *do you agree with that?* Perhaps a little analysis would help. First, it's clear from the Scriptures that our salvation has been made possible through Christ's work on the cross, not our human effort. God offers mankind eternal life as a gift, not as a reward, right? Second, if it were possible for me to lose my salvation, then God would have to reverse the transaction in some way, i.e., take back His gift or somehow strip me of His forgiveness, whatever. Then third, His Word would make that very clear so all of us could be adequately warned.

You see, if we start with God—as we certainly should—then we must say that He takes back the gift He said was ours, when we say we have lost our salvation. On top of that, the Bible would definitely include verses that explicitly state such facts.

Not only is it unthinkable that God would take back an eternal promise, it is impossible. Remember, He is immutable. That means He is unchanging. He cannot lie. Nor does He ever state that the gift of eternal life is on loan to us. On the contrary, Hebrews 10:14 clearly declares:

> *For by one offering He has perfected for all time those*
> *who are sanctified.*

The "one offering" refers to Christ's sacrificial death on the cross. And the result? We are told that "He has perfected FOR ALL TIME those who are sanctified." When we believe, when we take the gift of eternal life, we are set apart unto God, distinctly and uniquely His (sanctified), just as a new baby born into your home is set apart unto you. And God says it is a transaction that is in effect "for all time." No, there is nothing temporary in this arrangement.

You see, all the value of the finished work of Christ is placed by God to the credit of the sinner. Nothing can alter this. It is "for all time." Therefore, to suggest that the Christian's eternal acceptance is dependent upon his own conduct from one day to the next is really a slur upon the finished work of Christ. Actually, what that says is that Christ only began the work; you and I must finish it. If that were so, then we would deserve some of the glory. Nothing could be further from the truth!

SCRIPTURES EMPHASIZING GOD'S SECURE HOLD ON THE BELIEVER

Within the New Testament there are several passages worth consideration. Let's give attention to them for the next few minutes. Listen to 1 Corinthians 12:13:

> *For by one Spirit we were all baptized into one body,*
> *whether Jews or Greeks, whether slaves or free, and we were*
> *all made to drink of one Spirit.*

The Christian is said to be in the body, no matter his or her race or rank, and in full possession of the Spirit. If we could lose our salvation, we would certainly be expelled from the body. Yet no such idea is even *hinted* at in all the Bible. Not a single verse states that one who was once "in Christ" is now "out of Christ." This brings us to a promise Jesus gave while He was on earth:

> *All that the Father gives Me shall come to Me, and the*
> *one who comes to Me I will certainly not cast out (John 6:37).*

Just in case you're still struggling with the idea that salvation rests with God, not us, please observe that Jesus says it is the Father who gives us to the Son. Equally important, don't miss the fact that Jesus Himself stated that "the one who comes to Me I will certainly not cast out."

The Greek text declares a double negative—a highly emphatic statement that might be paraphrased "the one who comes to Me I will positively and absolutely not throw out." No "ifs," "ands," "buts," or "howevers" about it. This does not mean merely, "I will not reject or refuse," but also "I will not give up after receiving." Nothing temporary about that!

Now, consider Ephesians 1:13 and 4:30.

> *In Him, you also, after listening to the message of truth,*
> *the gospel of your salvation—having also believed, you were*
> *sealed in Him with the Holy Spirit of promise.*

> *And do not grieve the Holy Spirit of God, by whom you*
> *were sealed for the day of redemption.*

Not only does the Holy Spirit place us into the universal Body of Christ, He "seals" us. This seal goes into effect from the moment we believe. If we could lose our salvation, obviously that seal would have to be broken. But that would contradict God's promise. If He says we are sealed for the day of redemption (the day we receive new bodies that will last forever), then we can be certain nothing will interrupt that divine plan. Neither here nor anywhere else do the Scriptures speak of the Spirit's seal being broken—or loosened.

Romans 8:1 is also worth our attention:

> *There is therefore now no condemnation for those who*
> *are in Christ Jesus.*

And with that verse, Romans 8:31–39:

> *What then shall we say to these things? If God is for us,
> who is against us? He who did not spare His own Son, but
> delivered Him up for us all, how will He not also with Him
> freely give us all things? Who will bring a charge against God's
> elect? God is the one who justifies; who is the one who con-
> demns? Christ Jesus is He who died, yes, rather who was
> raised, who is at the right hand of God, who also intercedes for
> us. Who shall separate us from the love of Christ? Shall tribu-
> lation, or distress, or persecution, or famine, or nakedness, or
> peril, or sword? Just as it is written, "FOR THY SAKE WE
> ARE BEING PUT TO DEATH ALL DAY LONG; WE
> WERE CONSIDERED AS SHEEP TO BE SLAUGH-
> TERED." But in all these things we overwhelmingly conquer
> through Him who loved us. For I am convinced that neither
> death, nor life, nor angels, nor principalities, nor things pre-
> sent, nor things to come, nor powers, nor height, nor depth, nor
> any other created thing, shall be able to separate us from the
> love of God, which is in Christ Jesus our Lord.*

The strongest possible term for eternal punishment is translated "condemnation" in Romans 8:1. We are assured that we do
not face such punishment once we are "in Christ Jesus." And the
last section of Romans 8 further assures us that we have God on our
side!

Who will bring a charge against us? There is no accuser!

Who will condemn us? There is no judge!

Who will separate us from the love of Christ? There is no
executioner!

Why? Because we are secure in Christ Jesus. And if you look
closely, you will see that none of these promises are conditional.
God is for us (v. 31). We overwhelmingly conquer (v. 37). We are
enveloped, protected, safe, and secure against all possible threats
(vv. 38–39).

And our study of Scripture would be incomplete if we failed
to examine John 10:27–29:

My sheep hear My voice, and I know them, and they follow Me; and I give eternal life to them, and they shall never perish; and no one shall snatch them out of My hand. My Father, who has given them to Me, is greater than all; and no one is able to snatch them out of the Father's hand.

Read those words with discernment. Of whom is Jesus speaking? They are His followers. Christians. True believers. These verses do not talk about how a person becomes a sheep, but rather the results of being a sheep. Jesus is explaining that it is the Father's purpose to keep us secure in spite of everything and everyone!

Look closely. We are surrounded by a double wall of security. We are in Christ's eternal grip and "no one shall snatch them" out of Jesus' hand. And then He, in turn, states that we and He are in the Father's hand, making it absolutely impossible for anyone to be able "to snatch them out of the Father's hand."

Listen to 1 John 5:18b:

He who was born of God keeps him and the evil one does not touch him.

Notice the word *touch*. One reliable authority says the original Greek term means "to assault, in order to sever the vital union between Christ and the believer."[1] Not even the devil with all his supernatural power can assault the believer so as to sever our eternal union. Magnificent promise! Those who are born again are "kept" by Christ.

One final verse is deserving of our attention—the next-to-the-last verse in the letter of Jude:

Now to Him who is able to keep you from stumbling, and to make you stand in the presence of His glory blameless with great joy . . . (Jude 24).

The scene is that future day when the believer stands before Christ prior to entering into the glory of heaven. How shall we stand? Ashamed? Uncertain of our entrance? Insecure and seized by fear? No way! We are promised that He is the One who will make us stand "in the presence of His glory blameless with great joy." Blameless! What a promise for believers near death!

We have examined one scripture after another that carries the same theme. We have learned that our salvation really rests on God's strength, not ours. That our safety is in Christ's power, not ours. That our protection depends on the Father's firm grip, not ours. And that no one, including the devil, can sever the vital union that connects us with the Lord Jesus Christ. Why? Because it was His death and resurrection that perfected us "for all time" . . . because of His finished work, not ours.

WHY SOME DOUBT AND DENY

As we trace our way through these many passages (there are dozens more), you might begin to wonder how anyone could ever doubt and deny that the Christian is secure. Having spoken with some who struggle with this doctrine, I have discovered that most of them have difficulty in four areas: certain problem passages, fear that this will lead to loose living, a misunderstanding of carnality, and feelings of unworthiness. These deserve an answer.

Problem Passages

Admittedly, there are certain scriptures that seem, at first glance, to teach that Christians can drift so far from God that they are no longer in His family. Rather than taking the time to examine these, let me give you some guidelines to follow when you encounter such verses.

1. Read the words of the verse very carefully.

2. Study the "setting" or context of the verse.

3. Remember that God cannot contradict Himself. He certainly would not be saying one thing here and another thing elsewhere.

4. Pray for wisdom and insight.

5. Seek the counsel of resources—either reliable books or careful students of the Scriptures whom you admire. But mainly compare Scripture with Scripture.

6. If you still cannot understand, patiently wait for God to

show you in days to come. His Word is like a deep, deep mine, and some of its riches do not fall into our laps at the snap of our fingers.

Fear of Loose Living

Romans 6:1–11 declares a serious warning. Take the time to read these words:

> Well then, shall we keep on sinning so that God can keep on showing us more and more kindness and forgiveness? Of course not! Should we keep on sinning when we don't have to? For sin's power over us was broken when we became Christians and were baptized to become a part of Jesus Christ; through his death the power of your sinful nature was shattered. Your old sin-loving nature was buried with him by baptism when he died, and when God the Father, with glorious power, brought him back to life again, you were given his wonderful new life to enjoy. For you have become a part of him, and so you died with him, so to speak, when he died; and now you share his new life, and shall rise as he did. Your old evil desires were nailed to the cross with him; that part of you that loves to sin was crushed and fatally wounded, so that your sin-loving body is no longer under sin's control, no longer needs to be a slave to sin; for when you are deadened to sin you are freed from all its allure and its power over you. And since your old sin-loving nature "died" with Christ, we know that you will share his new life. Christ rose from the dead and will never die again. Death no longer has any power over him. He died once for all to end sin's power, but now he lives forever in unbroken fellowship with God. So look upon your old sin nature as dead and unresponsive to sin, and instead be alive to God, alert to him, through Jesus Christ our Lord (TLB).

Any doctrine can be abused, but that is hardly a reason to reject that doctrine. It is my personal conviction that a firm, calm belief in eternal security provides a greater motivation to live for Christ than fear of losing my salvation. Quite frankly, if the latter were true, all that would be necessary to rectify my problem would be to get saved again. And again. And again.

You see, if I know that I am secure in the Father's hand—and that my loose living would be met with His strong discipline—the impetus to walk in the light will be there at all times! Ask any Christian who has spent much time under the smarting rod of God. It is anything but pleasant. It is life's ultimate stress fracture.

Misunderstanding of Carnality

As I mentioned earlier, those who hold to an insecure salvation leave little or no room in their teaching for carnality. Yet the New Testament is replete with illustrations of believers who drifted away from the Lord. That's the whole point of the prodigal son story (Luke 15:11–24). The boy truly deserved to be cast out—but he wasn't. The father could have rejected the son—but he didn't.

Unpleasant though it may be, carnality is an option. It bears grave and grim consequences, but we are not to confuse it with a loss of salvation. According to 1 Corinthians 11:30–32, there were some believers in ancient Corinth who continued to live such carnal lives, God removed them from the earth. Yet even *that* discipline is not to be confused with condemnation.

> *For this reason many among you are weak and sick, and a number sleep. But if we judged ourselves rightly, we should not be judged. But when we are judged, we are disciplined by the Lord in order that we may not be condemned along with the world.*

Remember, we who have believed in Christ will never, ever be condemned (Romans 8:1).

Feelings of Unworthiness

If we adopted a human logic, this would be a very natural problem. But all the way through this chapter, we have resisted the human perspective. We have refused to rely on feelings or turn to logic for our answers.

Some days I do not "feel" married. But I am. There are days I do not "feel" like I am over fifty years old. But I am. And there are times I don't "feel" worthy of my family's love. But it is there in abundance. My feelings are often terribly unreliable. So are yours.

Remember the prodigal? After he came to his senses he returned to his dad and began his speech in all sincerity.

> And the son said to him, "Father, I have sinned against heaven and in your sight; I am no longer worthy to be called your son" (Luke 15:21).

But his faithful, gracious, forgiving, patient father interrupted that speech with sweeping actions of mercy and grace. He restored the worthless, undeserving, once-rebellious son to a place of significance in the family. Without reservation, the father hugged his son home . . . the same son who "felt" so unworthy.

Guilt does an awful number on us. It will lie to us and beat us into submission. It will convince us that God's promises really don't apply to us. It will yell so loudly we will mistake it for the voice of God. It will put us down, stomp on us, remove us from circulation, and create such deep stress fractures in our lives that we will begin to question our own sanity.

But the beauty of grace (our only permanent deliverance from guilt) is that it meets us where we are and gives us what we don't deserve.

> I acknowledged my sin to Thee,
> And my iniquity I did not hide;
> I said, "I will confess my transgressions to the LORD";
> And Thou didst forgive the guilt of my sin (Psalm 32:5).

Guilty child of God, look up. Refuse to let your guilt convince you of a lie. You are God's child if you have been born into His family. You do not need to be born again, again! You need to "acknowledge" your sinful way. You need to "confess the transgressions" of your life to your Lord. On the authority of His Word, I assure you that He will forgive your sin and remove the accompanying guilt.

Let me urge you to do that now!

AN OLD TESTAMENT EXAMPLE

Tucked away in the first book of the Bible is a remarkable story. It illustrates the truth of all we've been thinking about in this chapter. It's the age-old story of the flood in the days of Noah.

But rather than focusing our attention upon the forty days and nights of rain or the universal scope of the deluge, let's think about those eight people who were preserved from death. According to Genesis 7:7–10, Mr. and Mrs. Noah, plus their three sons and their sons' wives, along with the animals, entered the ark before the water of the flood began to rise upon the earth.

Those who have an eye for detail do not overlook a very significant part of the account. As the biblical record reveals the events that transpired just before the flood, the inspired writer makes an extremely important observation:

> So they went into the ark to Noah, by twos of all flesh in which was the breath of life. And those that entered, male and female of all flesh, entered as God had commanded him; and the Lord closed it behind him. Then the flood came upon the earth for forty days; and the water increased and lifted up the ark, so that it rose above the earth. And the water prevailed and increased greatly upon the earth; and the ark floated on the surface of the water (Genesis 7:15–18).

Did you catch the comment? We read that as soon as the animals and Noah with his family were in the ark as God had commanded, ". . . the LORD closed it behind him."

Who closed the door? The Lord.

Who was responsible for the security of all those lives? The Lord.

He personally saw to it that the righteous were safely locked inside. The fountains of the great deep burst open, and the floodgates of the sky split apart as never before or since. We cannot imagine the incredible scene of disaster that blasted the earth all around that tiny floating barge. But inside—removed from danger—there was divine security. The brevity of words highlights the magnificent keeping power of Almighty God.

. . . and only Noah was left, together with those that were with him in the ark (Genesis 7:23b).

No stress fractured their inner calm. No fear that they might sink. No sleepless nights, wondering if disaster would soon interrupt their peace and safety. No, we do not find a word in the record of any such thing. Why? Because *the Lord had closed them in*. Their security rested in His strength, not theirs. So we aren't surprised to read these words following the flood:

So Noah went out, and his sons and his wife and his sons' wives with him. Every beast, every creeping thing, and every bird, everything that moves on the earth, went out by their families from the ark (Genesis 8:18–19).

The One who had closed them in and preserved them through the disaster finally released them into an entirely new world, a fresh beginning.

That is exactly what He plans to do with us. The One who closed us in at the moment of our new birth is currently preserving us from any and all threats . . . and will some day release us into His eternal home. Blameless!

CONCLUDING COMFORT

With a sensitive eye on God's Word throughout this chapter, I have forged out my belief in the eternal security of the Christian. I find that this doctrine weaves its way peacefully and perfectly through the fabric of God's Word. Also, I find that the alternative position leaves little (if any) room for the large amount of teaching in the New Testament on the carnal Christian.

Candidly, if I did not believe that my salvation was eternally and permanently secure, I would be living my entire life without confidence and inner peace. I would forever wonder, "How far is too far?" In other words, if my salvation could be lost, I would never know if I had drifted too far. This would leave me in such a state of uneasiness that I seriously doubt if I could live one day free of worry. Terrible stress!

But being absolutely confident and comforted in the fact that my salvation is secure, based on God's keeping power, not mine, all cause for anxiety is removed. I may tremble on the Rock, but the Rock never trembles under me! And that inner assurance not only relieves my fear, it allows me to carry on with much greater efficiency. Rather than causing me to be indifferent and irresponsible, it inspires me to direct all my energies toward those things that please and glorify the name of my heavenly Father. I am eternally protected because He has me in His all-powerful hand.

In 1937, the famous Golden Gate Bridge was completed. At that time, it was the world's longest suspension bridge. The entire project cost the United States government $77 million. During the process of constructing the first section of the bridge, very few safety devices were used, resulting in twenty-three accidental deaths as workers fell helplessly into the waters far below.

The toll was so significant, something had to be done before the second section was built. An ingenious plan was arranged. The largest safety net in the world (it alone cost $100,000!) was made out of stout manila cordage and stretched out beneath the work crews. It proved to be an excellent investment in view of the fact that it saved the lives of at least ten men who fell into it without injury. Interestingly, the work went 25 percent faster, since the workers were relieved from the fear of falling to their deaths.

God's great net of security spans this globe. No matter where His children live, He has stretched out His everlasting arms beneath them. As a result, every one of us can live and work freely and fearlessly, knowing that we are protected, safe, secure, sealed, and kept by His power.

The anxiety and fear of perishing are gone. Eternal security has taken that great load off our minds.

As Linus once said, "Sound theology has a way of doing that."

———◦———

Faithful God of grace, Your Word is such a source of comfort. In a calm, clear manner it has spoken, leaving us encouraged. Thank You for replacing fear with confidence, for removing ignorance with reliable

information we needed to know. Thank you for sound theology!
Insecurity abounds. We don't know what tomorrow holds. We have no
absolute assurance that we'll be employed. Or have our health. Or enjoy
the presence of family and friends. Our lives are like a puff of smoke, as
uncertain as the morning fog. But one thing is certain. Being in Christ
is the safest place in life. And in calamity. And in death. In Him, and
in Him alone, we are secure. Eternally secure. And we are eternally
grateful . . . through Christ our Lord.

    Amen.

NOTES

Introduction

1. C.W. Havard, ed., *Black's Medical Dictionary*, 35th ed. (n.p.: B&N Imports), 1987.
2. Richard Demak, "The Pain That Won't Go Away," *Sports Illustrated*, 27 April 1987, pp. 60–71.
3. Ibid.

Chapter 1

1. Charles E. Hummel, *Tyranny of the Urgent!* (Downers Grove, Ill.: InterVarsity Christian Fellowship, 1967), p. 5.

Chapter 2

1. *Quote/Unquote*, compiled by Lloyd Cory (Wheaton, Ill.: Victor Books, 1977), p. 232.
2. Elisha A. Hoffman, "Leaning on the Everlasting Arms," *Hymns for the Family of God* (Nashville, Tenn.: Paragon Associates, Inc., 1976), p. 87.

Chapter 3

1. A. W. Tozer, *Root of the Righteous* (Harrisburg: Christian Publications, Inc., 1955), p. 137.
2. Gail MacDonald, *High Call, High Privilege* (Wheaton, Ill.: Tyndale House Publishers, Inc., 1981), p. 29.
3. M. Scott Peck, M.D., *The Road Less Traveled: A New Psychology of Love, Traditional Values, and Spiritual Growth* (New York: Touchstone Books, 1978), pp. 50–52, 56.

Chapter 4

1. Lord George Noel Gordon Byron, "Childe Harold's Pilgrimage," canto 4, stanza 10, in *Familiar Quotations*, ed. John Bartlett (Boston: Little, Brown & Co., 1955), pp. 453–54.
2. Alexander Whyte, *Bible Characters: The Old Testament* (London: Oliphants Ltd.; Grand Rapids, Mich.: Zondervan Publishing House, 1952), p. 382.

Chapter 5

1. John White, *The Fight* (Downers Grove, Ill.: InterVarsity Press, 1976), p. 179.
2. Charles W. Colson, *Loving God* (Grand Rapids, Mich.: Zondervan Publishing House, 1983), p. 131.
3. Kyle Yates, *Preaching from the Prophets* (North Nashville: Broadman Press, 1953), p. 152.
4. Karl Menninger, *Whatever Became of Sin?* (New York: Bantam Books, Inc., 1978), p. 138.
5. Jerry White, *Honesty, Morality, and Conscience* (Colorado Springs: NavPress, 1979), p. 184.
6. Quoted in Billy Graham, *World Aflame* (New York: Doubleday & Co., Inc., 1965), pp. 21–22.
7. John Brown, *Expository Discourses on 1 Peter* (Edinburgh: Banner of Truth, reprint edition, 1848), 1:106. Italics in original.
8. Graham, p. 23.
9. *The Works of Jonathan Edwards*, 2 vols., revised and corrected by Edward Hickman (Carlisle, Penn.: The Banner of Truth Trust, reprint edition, 1976), 1:XX. Italics in original.

Chapter 6

1. "Olympic Hockey Hero Craig Paid Price for Fame: an Ulcer," *Los Angeles Times*, 10 August 1980, Part III, p. 2.
2. F. B. Meyer, *Joseph* (Fort Washington, Penn.: Christian Literature Crusade, 1955), p. 30.
3. Dietrich Bonhoeffer, *Temptation* (London: SCM Press, 1964), p. 33.
4. Charles R. Swindoll, *Killing Giants, Pulling Thorns* (Portland, Ore.: Multnomah Press, 1978), p. 27.

Chapter 8

1. *The Real Mother Goose* (Chicago: Rand, McNally & Company, 1916), p. 26.
2. W. E. Vine, *An Expository Dictionary of New Testament Words*, vol. II (Westwood, N.J.: Fleming H. Revell Company, 1940), p. 248.
3. Samuel Taylor Coleridge, "Youth and Age," Stanza 2, *Familiar Quotations* (Boston: Little, Brown and Company, 1955), p. 425a.

Chapter 9

1. Leslie B. Flynn, *Man: Ruined & Restored* (Wheaton, Ill.: Victor Books, 1978), pp. 100–101.

Chapter 10

1. Merrill F. Unger, *Demons in the World Today* (Wheaton, Ill.: Tyndale House Publishers, 1971), p. 190.
2. Mark I. Bubeck, *The Adversary* (Chicago: Moody Press, 1975), p. 124. Used by permission of Moody Bible Institute.
3. Ibid., p. 125.

Chapter 11

1. Harold S. Kushner, *When Bad Things Happen to Good People* (New York: Schocken Books, 1981), p. 6.
2. Leighton Ford, "Yes, God Is Good," *Decision*, June 1982, p. 5.
3. Ibid.
4. Walter A. Henrichsen, *After the Sacrifice* (Grand Rapids: Zondervan Publishing House, 1979), p. 83.
5. Kushner, p. 26.
6. Source unknown.
7. Diane Ball, "In His Time," ©1978 by Maranatha Music. All rights reserved. International copyright secured. Used by permission.

Chapter 12

1. J. Grant Howard, Jr., *Knowing God's Will—and Doing It!* (Grand Rapids: Zondervan Publishing House, 1976), pp. 14, 15, 16. Used by permission.
2. Joseph A. Callaway, "Sir Flinders Petrie, Father of Palestinian Archaeology," *Biblical Archaeology Review* 6 (November/December 1980):51.

Chapter 13

1. W. E. Vine, *An Expository Dictionary of New Testament Words*, vol. 4 (Westwood, N.J.: Fleming H. Revell Company, 1940), p. 145.

A condensed edition of this book
is available on audio cassette.